Russia

Russia

By Nel Yomtov

Enchantment of the World™
Second Series

Children's Press®

An Imprint of Scholastic Inc.

New York   Toronto   London   Auckland   Sydney
Mexico City   New Delhi   Hong Kong
Danbury, Connecticut

Frontispiece: Domes on St. Basil's Cathedral, Moscow

Consultant: Hiroaki Kuromiya, Professor, Department of History, Indiana University, Bloomington, Indiana

Please note: All statistics are as up-to-date as possible at the time of publication.

Book production by The Design Lab

Library of Congress Cataloging-in-Publication Data

Yomtov, Nelson.
  Russia/by Nel Yomtov.
      p. cm.—(Enchantment of the world. Second series)
  Includes bibliographical references and index.
  ISBN: 978-0-531-27545-0 (lib. bdg.)
  1. Russia (Federation)—Juvenile literature. I. Title.
  DK510.23.Y66 2012
  947—dc23   2012000520

1 2 3 4 5 6 7 8 9 10 R 22 21 20 19 18 17 16 15 14 13

Russia

Contents

Cover photo:
Military parade in
Red Square

Mount Elbrus

Arctic fox

The Russian Giant

8

A QUICK LOOK AT A MAP OF THE WORLD WILL tell you that Russia is the largest nation. About twice the size of the United States, Russia sprawls across the continents of Asia and Europe. Its vast expanse stretches from the Baltic Sea, across northern Europe, through central Asia, and on to the Pacific Ocean.

Within this great expanse is an enormous variety of land features and climates. Flat plains stretch thousands of miles, enormous mountain ranges rise majestically into the skies, and broad rivers and deep lakes dot the Russian landscape. In the northern arctic regions, people struggle against subzero temperatures and bitterly frigid winds. In the south, mild temperatures provide farmers a good climate to grow crops.

Russia is one of the world's most multiethnic nations. Russians belong to more than one hundred ethnic groups, speak dozens of languages, and practice many different religions.

Opposite: **Russia includes about one-eighth of all the land on Earth.**

The Russian Giant **9**

Today, Russia is known as the Russian Federation. It is the largest of the independent states to survive the breakup of the Union of Soviet Socialist Republics (USSR or Soviet Union) in 1991. The USSR was formed in the early twentieth century by the Bolshevik Party, which became the Communist Party. The USSR was a Communist nation, in which the state owned most of the land and controlled the economy. The rise of Communists in Russia ended centuries of dominating rule by leaders called czars.

Bolshevik supporters attack the Winter Palace, the official home of the czar, during the Russian Revolution in 1917.

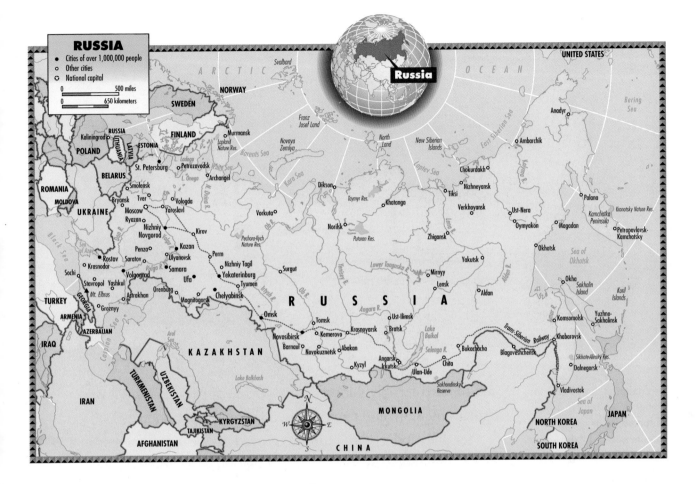

The czars had enjoyed lives of luxury and unimaginable wealth. They built ornate golden-domed palaces, churches, theaters, and concert halls. They dressed in fine furs, lush velvets, and glittering jewels. They attended magnificent parties in grand ballrooms.

The lavish lifestyle of the rich was made possible by the hard work and backbreaking toil of peasants and serfs who worked the land for the wealthy nobles. These workers did not own land

Beginning in the 1920s, the Soviet Union built a series of forced labor camps in remote parts of the country. Both political prisoners and criminals were sent to these prison camps.

and suffered terribly during Russia's frequent periods of civil war, foreign invasion, and famine, when there was not enough food.

Yet life under Communism proved to be equally oppressive as life under the czars. The population grew angry over the crumbling economy and a lack of personal freedoms. Communist leaders were brutal to those people they believed were unsupportive. In the early twentieth century, millions of Russians were imprisoned, executed, or sent to distant lands.

In the mid-twentieth century, the USSR grew to be a world superpower, building large numbers of nuclear weapons. The USSR and the United States engaged each other in a hostile period called the Cold War, which lasted from the late 1940s to the late 1980s. During that time, the Soviets made their mark on the world stage. The USSR became the first nation to venture into space, and Russian athletes emerged as many of the best in the world.

In the late twentieth century, the Soviet Union began to change. Several political and economic reforms begun by Mikhail Gorbachev, the leader of the Soviet Union, created a sense of political freedom within the nation. The easing of Communist rule in Russia and throughout Eastern Europe ultimately led to the breakup of the Soviet Union.

Mikhail Gorbachev worked to bring greater freedom to the Soviet Union.

The road to political freedom and economic stability was not easy following the collapse of the USSR. Russia had to deal with a tough economy, environmental pollution, homelessness, corruption, and organized crime. But in recent years, significant changes have been seen throughout society and government. These changes include a stronger economy, greater freedom of speech, and a rebirth of religious and artistic freedoms.

As the Russian people continue to seek greater personal freedom and prosperity, the world will keep a watchful eye on this giant in the decades ahead.

Across Two Continents

RUSSIA IS THE LARGEST COUNTRY IN THE WORLD, covering roughly 6.6 million square miles (17 million square kilometers). It spreads across Europe and Asia for 5,600 miles (9000 km), spanning nine time zones. About 25 percent of Russia lies in Europe, and the rest is in Asia. The mainland of eastern Russia lies only about 53 miles (85 km) across the Bering Strait from the U.S. state of Alaska.

European Russia

The Ural Mountains stretch north to south for roughly 1,550 miles (2,500 km) from the Kara Sea to Kazakhstan, creating a border between Europe and Asia. The mountains are generally low, with peaks rising to 3,000 feet (900 meters) above sea level. The Urals are an important area for mining and iron and steel production. Significant deposits of petroleum, coal, copper, tin, gold, lead, and asbestos are found in the Urals. The islands of Novaya Zemlya, once used as a site for nuclear weapons testing, are also part of the Urals range. They are located in the frigid Arctic, north of the mainland.

Russia's Geographic Features

Latitude and Longitude of Geographic Center: Near Novosibirsk, 55°01' N and 82°56' E

Area: 6.6 million square miles (17 million sq km)

Highest Elevation: Mount Elbrus, 18,510 feet (5,642 m) above sea level

Lowest Elevation: Caspian Sea, 92 feet (28 m) below sea level

Longest River: Lena, 2,734 miles (4,400 km)

Largest Lake: Lake Baikal, 12,248 square miles (31,722 sq km)

Highest Recorded Temperature: 111°F (44°C), Yashkul, Kalmykia Republic, July 11, 2010

Lowest Recorded Temperature: -90°F (-68°C), Oymyakon (February 6, 1933) and Verkhoyansk (February 7, 1892) near the Arctic Circle

Average High Temperature: In St. Petersburg, 26°F (-3°C) in January, 73°F (23°C) in July

Average Low Temperature: In St. Petersburg, 18°F (-8°C) in January, 59°F (15°C) in July

Average Annual Precipitation: Precipitation across the East European Plain averages from 24 to 28 inches (61 to 71 cm), up to 39 inches (99 cm) in the southern areas of the Russian Far East, and 79 inches (200 cm) in the western mountains.

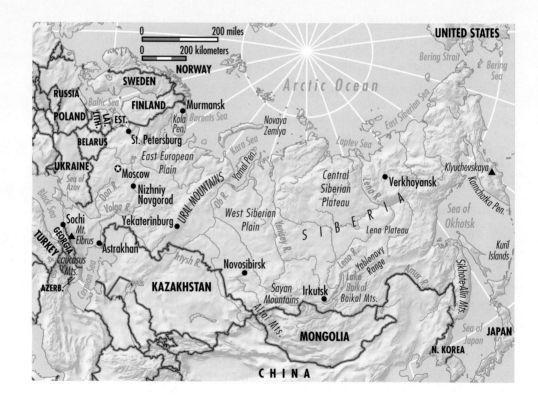

The East European Plain is located in the part of Russia that lies west of the Ural Mountains. The land is generally flat and open, making it suitable for agriculture. The East European Plain accounts for only about 25 percent of Russia's total land area, but it is home to about 80 percent of Russia's population. The nation's two largest cities—Moscow and St. Petersburg—lie within the East European Plain.

Much of the northern European Plain is covered with forests and lakes. The forestland provides a steady source of timber, fish, and animal furs. The soil in the southern region is better suited for growing crops, such as rye, wheat, barley, and potatoes.

Cabbage grows well on the East European Plain. Russia is the third-largest cabbage producer in the world.

Mount Elbrus is a volcano, but it is not active. Its last eruption took place about two thousand years ago.

In the northwest of the European Plain is the mountainous Kola Peninsula, which borders the Barents and the White Seas, branches of the Arctic Ocean. The area is rich in oil and gas deposits and minerals. Murmansk is the largest city on the peninsula, with a population of more than three hundred thousand. The region was settled as early as 300 BCE.

The Caucasus Mountains form the southern edge of the East European Plain. These rocky, snowcapped peaks stretch about 500 miles (800 km) between the Black and Caspian Seas. In the north Caucasus, Mount Elbrus, the tallest peak in Europe, rises to a dizzying height of 18,510 feet (5,642 m). In the southern region, the Don River flows into the Black Sea. It is an important trade route because it connects the European Plain with the Black Sea through the Sea of Azov.

Mother Volga

Flowing a total of 2,294 miles (3,692 km), the Volga is the longest river in Europe. Often called *Volga mat*, or "Mother Volga," by the Russian people, it is essential to the Russian way of life. More than 40 percent of the Russian population lives near it, and roughly half of Russia's farmers grow crops near the Volga.

The river rises in the Valdai Hills northwest of Moscow and meanders east and then south across the East European Plain. It empties into the Caspian Sea near Astrakhan in southern European Russia. The delta of the Volga provides an excellent environment for wildlife. More than two hundred species of birds visit the delta during the mild summer months.

Many dams have been built along the Volga, creating some of the world's largest reservoirs. The reservoirs hold about half of the Volga's water, much of which is used for irrigation. The flowing water is also used to turn turbines, which make hydroelectric power.

The Volga is a major water route, carrying about half of all river freight in Russia. A series of canals and other constructed waterways connect the Volga to other bodies of water. For example, the Volga-Baltic Waterway links the Volga with the Baltic Sea.

Wheat is grown in the Volga's fertile valley, which is also rich in minerals, natural gas, salt, and potash, used in fertilizers. The valley is also home to a large oil industry.

Development along the Volga has created significant pollution problems. Factory and household wastes combine with fertilizer and pesticide runoff from farms to harm life in the river. People wash cars and farm equipment in the river, polluting the waterway with oil and grease. Only in recent years has the government taken steps to halt the effects of pollution.

The Volga River begins northwest of Moscow, crossing the East European Plain along the foothills of the Ural Mountains, as it makes its way toward the Caspian Sea. Like the Don River, the Volga has been an important highway of commerce for centuries.

Sochi, in the south European Plain, is a resort city on the Black Sea coast. Each year, about two million people spend their summer vacations on Sochi's sand and pebble beaches, enjoying the resort's parks, monuments, and architecture.

Siberia is dotted with lakes of all sizes.

Asian Russia

Siberia is a vast mass of land east of the Ural Mountains. It stretches all the way to the Pacific Ocean in the east and from the Arctic Ocean south to China, Mongolia, and Kazakhstan. Siberia's diverse landscape features plateaus, massive mountain ranges, and broad rolling plains. There is no shortage of water in the region: Siberia has more than twenty-three thousand rivers and more than one million lakes.

Directly east of the Urals is the marshy West Siberian Plain. This flat landscape of forests, swamps, and lakes extends east to the 2,540-mile-long (4,090 km) Yenisey River. In the north, the Yamal Peninsula pokes into the Kara Sea, north of the Arctic Circle. The towering Altai and Sayan Mountains lie on the southern border of the West Siberian Plain.

In addition to the Yenisey River, two other major river systems wind their way across this plain. The Ob River begins in the Altai Mountains and then zigzags northwest across the middle of the West Siberian Plain. It empties into the Kara Sea by way of the Gulf of Ob. The Irtysh River flows 2,640 miles (4,249 km) north from Kazakhstan before joining the Ob River.

Some of the world's largest reserves of oil and natural gas are found in the West Siberian Plain. During the 1970s and 1980s, most of the Soviet Union's gas production came from this region. Because swamps and marshlands make up much of the area, and portions of the plains flood in the spring, large sections of the West Siberian Plain are unsuitable for agriculture.

Looking at Russia's Cities

Moscow, the capital of Russia, is also the country's largest city. In 2010, Moscow had an estimated population of 11.5 million people. St. Petersburg (right), Russia's second-largest city, is located on the Neva River at the west end of the Baltic Sea. It has a population of 4,848,700 people. Russian czar Peter the Great founded the city in 1703, and for the next fifteen years it served as the capital of Russia. The city is made up of many islands that are connected by bridges. The State Hermitage Museum complex, generally referred to as simply the Hermitage, is one of the world's great museums. It stretches along the Palace Embankment. This street in central St. Petersburg also contains the Winter Palace, once the official residence of Russian empresses and czars, and the Marble Palace. The city is a major tourist attraction, with more than two hundred museums, two thousand libraries, one hundred concert halls, and forty-five galleries and exhibition halls.

Russia's third-largest city, Novosibirsk, is the largest city in Siberia, with a population of 1,473,737. It was founded in 1893 along the tracks of the Trans-Siberian Railway, making the city an important transportation center in the region. The average high temperature there in January is 10°F (-12°C), but temperatures warm to a mild 78°F (26°C) in July. Some of the city's major industries produce electricity, gas, and water. Saint Alexander Nevsky Cathedral opened in 1899. It was built as a tribute to Emperor Alexander III and is one of the first stone buildings constructed in Novosibirsk. The world-renowned Novosibirsk Zoo and the Opera and Ballet Theater (left) are popular destinations.

Yekaterinburg is Russia's fourth-largest city. It was founded in 1723 and has a population of 1,350,136. It was named after Peter the Great's wife, Empress Catherine I, whose name in Russian is Yekaterina. Located on the border of Europe and Asia, Yekaterinburg lies on the eastern side of the Ural Mountains on the Iset River. Machinery and metal processing are the city's main industries. Yekaterinburg is noted for its theaters and theater companies, including the Academic Dramatic Theater, the Theater for Young Spectators, and the State Academic Opera and Ballet Theater.

Farther east is the Central Siberian Plateau, a deeply eroded land. It extends from the Yenisey River in the west to the Lena River valley in the east. The Central Siberian Plateau is a rich source of natural gas and minerals such as gold, coal, iron ore, diamonds, and platinum. Oil and natural gas fields extend from the Lena Plateau in the east to the city of Irkutsk near Lake Baikal in the south.

The plateau's largest river is the Lena River. It starts in the Baikal Mountains, 4 miles (7 km) west of Lake Baikal. Many people believe that the Russian Communist revolutionary

Oil is plentiful in parts of northern Russia. Workers are building an oil pipeline across eastern Siberia to the Pacific. From there, the oil can be shipped to other countries.

Greatest Lake

Lake Baikal, the world's largest freshwater lake, lies between the Sayan and Yablonovy ranges. Covering an area of 12,248 square miles (31,722 sq km) with depths up to 5,387 feet (1,642 m), it contains more water than all of North America's Great Lakes combined. More than 1,500 species of plant and animal life are found only at Lake Baikal and nowhere else on Earth. Baikal is the oldest lake in the world, having formed more than thirty million years ago.

Vladimir Ilyich Ulyanov took the name "Lenin" from the Lena River, because he had once been exiled to the Central Siberian Plateau.

To the east is the Russian Far East, which extends from the Lena River valley in the west to the Pacific Ocean in the east. The region is a wilderness of plateaus, mountains, and woodlands, with large areas of permafrost, or permanently frozen ground.

Russia's Pacific coastline extends south from the Bering Sea to the Sea of Okhotsk to the Sea of Japan. It is more than 10,000 miles long (16,000 km). The landscape changes from permafrost in the north to lush forests in the south.

The Kamchatka Peninsula, which juts into the Sea of Okhotsk, is home to about two hundred volcanoes, of which roughly thirty are active. The highest peak in the Kamchatka chain is Klyuchevskaya, standing at 15,863 feet (4,835 m). Kronotsky Nature Reserve in southeastern Kamchatka has more than two hundred geysers, which spew out fountains of hot, steamy water. Yellowstone National Park in the United States is the only place in the world with more geysers than Kronotsky. Extending from the southern tip of the Kamchatka Peninsula are the scenic Kuril Islands, a range of underwater volcanoes. They separate the Sea of Okhotsk from the Pacific Ocean.

The Sikhote-Alin Mountains in the south of the Russian Far East have a warm and wet climate. Thick dense forests grow there. The region is home to many animals, including the rare Siberian tiger. The Sikhote-Alin chain extends roughly 900 miles (1,450 km) southwest to northeast along the coast of the Sea of Japan.

Wildfire!

In 2010, hundreds of wildfires broke out in western Russia, causing widespread destruction. Beginning in May, unusually high temperatures were experienced in the Sakha Republic in the Far Eastern region. The warming pattern moved westward to the Ural Mountains and finally settled in European Russia by July.

Massive wildfires erupted from late July through early September. The blazes, fueled by widespread drought, devastated villages, farmland, and woodlands. More than two thousand buildings were destroyed. In large urban areas, the heat wave along with the blanket of choking smog produced by the fires killed thousands of people.

Large tracts of dry land contributed to the wildfires in the Moscow area. In the 1960s, swamps and bogs had been drained so the areas could be used for agriculture and to mine peat as a fuel source. In 2002, a series of wildfires taught people that in order to prevent such fires these drained areas needed to be rewatered. However, this was not done. As a result, the dry peat fields were a factor in the 2010 wildfires that blazed out of control for weeks.

Russian winters bring frigid
temperatures and sometimes
heavy snow.

Climate

Because of its enormous size, Russia has a wide range of
climates. The frigid seas in the north create arctic and sub-
arctic zones where the average winter temperature is -56°
Fahrenheit (-49° Celsius). With no mountains to protect
against the cold arctic weather, northern cities feel the bitter
sting of a long winter. Winter is Russia's longest season, last-
ing from November to mid-April in some places. The winter
months are marked by heavy frosts, ice, and snowstorms. St.
Petersburg can be covered in snow for as many as 150 days a
year, and rivers in Siberia may remain frozen for more than
225 days a year.

In the south and in the Caucasus, summer temperatures
can soar to 108°F (42°C). Moist air from the ocean prevents

extremes of hot and cold and warms European Russia. Regions farther away from the water have long winters and short, dry summers.

East of the Ural Mountains and up into the Arctic Circle, winter blizzards bury the land under snow for most of the year. Many of the world's coldest places are located in eastern Siberia, where temperatures can reach lows of -93°F (-69°C). Verkhoyansk has an average high temperature in January of -46°F (-43°C). But even Siberia warms up in the summer, and summer highs in Verkhoyansk reach 73°F (23°C). Russia's most moderate temperatures are generally found in the southwest, especially along the coasts of the Caspian and Black Seas.

Children enjoy a refreshing romp in a fountain on a warm day in Moscow.

Tundra, Taiga, Forest, Steppe

THE VAST RUSSIAN LANDSCAPE FEATURES FOUR BROAD zones, or ecosystems: tundra, taiga, forest, and steppe. Each zone stretches west to east across the nation, and each supports its own unique mix of plant and animal life.

Opposite: **Tundra covers much of the Kamchatka Peninsula in eastern Russia.**

Tundra

The northernmost region of Russia is the tundra, where the ground is permafrost. This is when the soil just a few inches below the ground surface is frozen year-round. Stretching along the shores of the Arctic Ocean, the tundra runs from the Kola Peninsula in the west all the way east to the Bering Sea.

The tundra is covered with snow for ten or eleven months a year. The top layers of soil thaw in the summer. During this time, scrubby mosses, short grasses, and lichens grow. Trees cannot grow in the tundra because they are unable to sink their roots into the permafrost. In summer, the melted snow creates marshes and pools, where mosquitoes thrive.

Only the hardiest animal species can survive the harsh environment of the tundra. On land, arctic foxes, oxen, and

Permafrost

Permafrost is ground that is always frozen. This occurs in regions where the average air temperature is continually below 32°F (0°C), the temperature at which the water and moisture in the soil freezes. Only the upper layers of permafrost thaw in summer. Permafrost can vary between several hundred feet and several thousand feet deep.

Permafrost covers about half the land in Russia. In regions with permafrost, it can be difficult to mine or build. After a building is constructed on permafrost, the heat from the building begins to thaw the ground below. The ground becomes soft and muddy, and the structure sinks into the ground.

lemmings roam the tundra. In the summer, herds of reindeer feed on the sparse vegetation that covers the ground. Seals and walruses live in the frigid northern seas, feeding on fish. Snowy owls and ravens also live in the region, and during the short summer months, flocks of ducks, geese, and swans nest in the tundra.

Taiga

South of the tundra is an enormous belt of evergreen forest called the taiga. It covers roughly the other half of Russia that is not tundra. Spanning Russia from the Baltic Sea to the Pacific Ocean, the taiga is the world's largest forest. Trees

In summer, the arctic fox has brown fur. In winter, the fur turns white so it blends in with the snow.

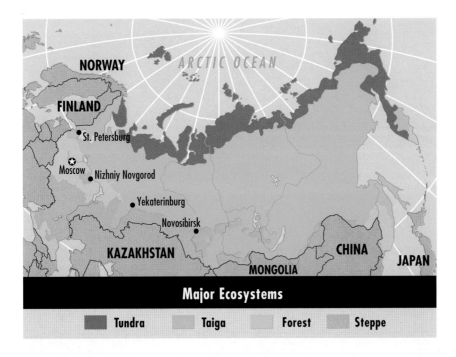

Tundra	**Taiga**	**Forest**	**Steppe**

grow on the taiga because the permafrost begins deeper in the ground there and the milder climate provides longer growing seasons. Evergreen trees such as pine, fir, and spruce grow in the taiga. Larch trees, which grow needles in the summer before dropping their leaves in the fall, are also common.

Symbol of the Nation

The brown bear is the national symbol of Russia. Brown bears have long, thick fur and a mane at the back of the neck. They can weigh up to 1,700 pounds (770 kilograms) and run 30 miles per hour (50 kph). Their blunt, curved claws are sometimes 4 inches (10 cm) long.

Brown bears eat berries, roots, and sprouts, as well as fish, insects, and small mammals. Exceptionally strong swimmers, some Russian brown bears feed mainly on salmon, which gives them the nutrients to grow large.

Adult males can be very aggressive. During fights, the bears strike each other in the chest or shoulders and try to bite each other's head or neck.

Vast forests stretch across
Siberia. Nearly a quarter
of the world's forest lies in
Russia.

Wildlife on the forested portions of the taiga includes sables, which belong to the weasel family. For centuries, Russian fur trappers have hunted sables in order to sell the animals' fur, which is used to manufacture hats and coats. Brown bears, elks, and foxes also roam the woodlands. Smaller animals on the taiga include squirrels, ermines, and muskrats.

Forest

The taiga gradually transforms into the forest zone, the next band to the south. This zone is widest on the European side and becomes narrower toward the Ural Mountains. The forest is a mix of cone trees, such as pine and spruce, and trees that drop their leaves in the fall, such as oak, birch, and maple. Large portions of the forest, especially in European Russia, have been cleared for farming and industry.

Because of this deforestation and the pollution caused by industrial development, wildlife does not thrive in the forest zone. Wolves, foxes, squirrels, and roe deer are still common, however.

Steppe

To the south of the mixed forest is the steppe, a region consisting mainly of flat plains and grasslands. The steppe stretches eastward from European Russia in the west, past the Ural

Back from the Brink

The Siberian tiger is one of the world's rarest animals. It lives mainly along the Amur and Ussuri Rivers in the Sikhote-Alin Mountains in the Russian Far East. Its fur is a reddish-orange or reddish-yellow color, with narrow black stripes. The average male grows from 9 to 12 feet (3 to 4 m) long and can weigh between 400 and 650 pounds (180 and 295 kg). Females are smaller.

Tigers feed on musk deer, Manchurian wapiti, and goral, which are small goatlike animals that live on rocky hillsides. Smaller prey includes rabbits, hares, salmon, and small rodents called pikas.

By the early twentieth century, the Siberian tiger had been hunted nearly to extinction. But in 1947, tiger hunting was outlawed. By that time, only twenty to thirty Siberian tigers remained. Since then, the Siberian tiger has made a remarkable comeback. Today, an estimated 350 to 400 tigers live in the Far East region.

Mountains, all the way to the Yenisey River in the Siberian Plain. Its rich black soil is the most fertile in Russia. Fruits, vegetables, wheat, sugar beets, barley, and sunflowers grow in abundance on the steppe.

In the northern steppe, forests of birch, spruce, oak, and ash provide a home to deer, wild boar, and mink. The center band of the steppe is farmland, where mild temperatures support animal life such as antelopes, squirrels, mice, and hamsters. Geese and egrets live in the Volga River basin.

Wild boars will eat anything they find. They regularly eat grass, roots, nuts, berries, insects, and reptiles.

The National Tree

The white birch tree is the national tree of Russia. It grows mainly in the taiga and forest. The bark of the birch has provided countless uses throughout the centuries. In ancient Russia, the bark was used as writing paper. It was also used to make shoes, utensils, and waterproof containers. Parents often carved birch bark trinkets or figures for their children, to ward off evil spirits. Today, many Russian artisans craft handsome decorative boxes from the bark of the birch tree.

The southern edge of the steppe in European Russia is marked by the Caucasus Mountains, a range that contains some of Russia's highest peaks. Roughly 1,600 of the 6,400 different types of plants found in the mountains grow only in Russia. Leopards, wolves, European bison, lynx, and hedgehogs make their homes in the hills. Birds in the Caucasus include golden eagles and hooded crows. The snake-like glass lizard also lives in the region. It can drop off part of its tail to distract predators. When it falls off, the tail breaks into several pieces. Eventually, a smaller tail will grow back on the lizard.

Golden eagles are powerful predators.

The Sweep of History

THOUSANDS OF YEARS AGO, NOMADIC PEOPLES LIVED on the Russian plains and in eastern Europe. In about 300 CE, a group of people called Eastern Slavs began migrating westward. The areas they settled were near what is now Moscow and what eventually became Belarus and Ukraine. They founded important towns that include Kiev and Novgorod. By 600, their community, which came to be called the Rus, thrived as traders, trappers, and farmers.

Opposite: **Vladimir I, shown in this statue in Novgorod, made Christianity the state religion of Kievan Rus.**

Kievan Rus

Attracted by the prosperity of the Rus, invaders from Scandinavia called the Varangians, or Vikings, raided and conquered many Eastern Slav villages. Around 862, a Varangian adventurer named Rurik conquered Novgorod and became leader of the Eastern Slavs living there. Oleg, Rurik's successor, captured Kiev in 882. He established a state called Kievan Rus, which blossomed into one of Europe's wealthiest territories.

In 988, Vladimir I, the ruler of Kievan Rus, joined the Greek Orthodox Church and made Christianity the official

Ancient Finds

Prehistoric Russia was the home to many ancient peoples. In the Denisova Cave of the Altai Mountains in southwestern Siberia, scientists have discovered bone fragments of early humanlike beings that date back forty thousand years. Remains of sixty-six species of mammals, fifty species of birds, and remnants of reptiles have been found in the cave. Tools and decorative objects made by Neanderthals have also been found in the cave. These ancient artifacts are made of bone, animal teeth, ostrich egg shells, and the tusks of large elephantine animals called mammoths.

Among the artifacts found on the Ukok Plateau, which is also located in the Altai Mountains, is a 2,400-year-old frozen mummy of a woman nicknamed the Ice Maiden. The woman was discovered in 1993 (right). She was buried in a large wooden coffin in a tomb containing six sacrificed horses, saddles, wool rugs, and containers of food. The young blond woman was dressed in a long wool skirt, a gold-adorned silk blouse, and white felt stockings. Her body was covered with ornate tattoos of animals. Scientists believe that she might have been a warrior chief or priestess because of her elaborate burial arrangements.

religion of Kievan Rus. The Greek Orthodox Church had a wide range of influence. It was based in Constantinople, the capital of the Byzantine Empire. This empire stretched across southern Europe, western Asia, and North Africa. This marked the beginnings of the powerful Russian Orthodox Church.

Members of the royal family of Kievan Rus became bitter rivals. They battled one another for control of land and power in Kiev and smaller cities and towns. Rather than being ruled by a central leader in Kiev, the state broke into separate principalities, smaller territories ruled by princes. Trade was destroyed, and the people suffered from hunger and poverty.

The internal struggles weakened Kievan Rus and made it vulnerable to attacks from outsiders.

The Golden Horde

In the 1200s, skilled horsemen and warriors called the Mongols swept through Russia from the south. Led by Genghis Khan, they established a powerful empire that crossed Asia and spread westward toward Europe. The Slavs called the invaders Tatars, and they were commonly known as the Golden Horde.

In 1237, Batu Khan, grandson of Genghis, destroyed dozens of Russian cities, including Moscow and Kiev. By 1240, Russia had become part of the vast Mongol Empire.

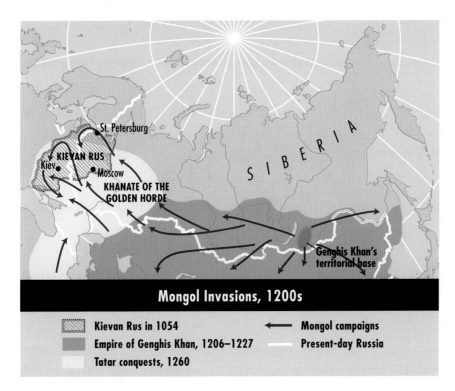

Mongol Invasions, 1200s

▨ Kievan Rus in 1054	← Mongol campaigns
▨ Empire of Genghis Khan, 1206–1227	— Present-day Russia
▨ Tatar conquests, 1260	

The Mongols first invaded Kievan Rus in 1223.

The Mongols did not occupy the Rus territories they conquered. Instead, they allowed local rulers to remain in power. But the Tatars demanded tribute, or taxes. Rus princes and their subjects also had to serve in the Mongol army. The Mongols appointed Russian rulers and hired foreign agents to collect taxes.

The Rise of Muscovy

Under the Tatars, the principality of Muscovy, later called Moscow, prospered and grew into an important region. Located on a major trade route, Muscovy rivaled Kiev and Novgorod as an economic and social center. By the early 1300s, Muscovy had become the most powerful principality. As a sign of the city's newfound importance, the Russian Orthodox Church moved its headquarters from Kiev to Muscovy.

In the late fourteenth century, Russian princes began to resist their Tatar masters. They battled the Mongols but remained under their control. In the late fifteenth century, the grand prince of Muscovy, Ivan III, known as Ivan the Great (1440–1505), gained control over many nobles. He began to bring the former Rus territories together again. Backed by this new power, in 1480,

Ivan the Great riding in a sleigh. He ruled Russia for forty-three years.

Ivan the Great tears up a letter from the leader of the Tatars, showing his refusal to pay them tribute.

he refused to pay any more tribute to the Mongols. This bold move broke the Tatars' hold on the Russians.

The First Czars

Ivan the Great was the first ruler to call himself czar. He took the title First Czar of All the Russias, becoming the ruler of all the Rus people. He took control of the principalities of Novgorod and Tver and continued to strengthen Moscow. During his reign, Ivan III transformed the concept of land ownership in Russia. Before him, nobles owned land completely. Under his laws, nobles could not own land unless it was used for military and government service to the czar. Another rule established that the landlord was entitled to part of the crops that peasants grew on the land.

The military victories of Ivan IV (1530–1584), Ivan the Great's grandson, expanded Russian territories. Russia now stretched south to the Caspian Sea and east across the Ural Mountains to Siberia. Ivan IV was known as Ivan the Terrible because he had a vicious temper and murdered political opponents.

Ivan IV created a national assembly, which he controlled in order to weaken the nobles. His secret police force was created to take control of the estates of wealthy landowners, or aristocrats, called boyars. It was also used to control Russian peasants or serfs who worked and lived on Russian estates, usually under brutal conditions.

Serfs worked hard for landowners. They were not allowed to move, and if they ran away they could be captured and returned to the nobles.

During Michael Romanov's reign, order was restored to Russia, and the country made peace with Sweden and Poland.

In 1598, the other son of Ivan the Terrible died without an heir. This plunged Russia into the "Time of Troubles." This was an era when czars tried to strengthen the aristocracy's stranglehold on the nation. The state claimed the right to control private property, and the independence of the church was threatened. Oppression, violence, civil unrest, and famine dominated Russia.

Finally, in 1613, the national assembly met to select a new czar. They chose Michael Romanov, a sixteen-year-old nobleman. Starting with Michael, the Romanov family would rule Russia for three hundred years.

In 1682, ten-year-old Peter I (1672–1725) became czar, along with his half-brother Ivan V. When Ivan died in 1689, Peter became the sole czar and instituted a series of major changes that reshaped Russia. He became known as Peter the Great.

Peter traveled throughout Europe studying Western industry and military technology. He built a powerful army and created a navy to help expand Russian territory to the Baltic Sea in order to gain a shipping port. Factories were soon springing up throughout Russia. They manufactured weapons, textiles, and other goods. Joining forces with Poland and Denmark, Peter captured

Peter the Great is credited with modernizing Russia and making it into a powerful European state.

Swedish territories, and he founded St. Petersburg in 1703. In 1709, Russia defeated the Swedes at the Battle of Poltava, ending the Swedish threat to Russia's newly won territories.

Although Russia was modernizing and on its way to becoming a world power, there was great unrest among the peasants. Serfdom had been legalized, and factory owners were allowed to buy peasants as workers, essentially enslaving them. High taxes were placed on the Russian people but not on nobles and church leaders. Peter the Great made education a require-

Wealthy Russians enjoyed a life of luxury, but the vast majority of Russians were poor peasants.

ment for children of the nobility but not for peasant children. The prospering Russian Empire was doing nothing to improve the conditions of the common people.

Catherine the Great

In 1762, Peter the Great's grandson, Peter III, became czar. He was soon assassinated, and his German wife, Catherine II, assumed the throne. She became known as Catherine the Great.

Catherine continued to expand Russia, using both warfare and politics. During her reign, eastern Poland, Lithuania, Belarus, western Ukraine, and Crimea came under Russian control. The Russian Empire now stretched from the Baltic Sea to the Pacific Ocean.

Catherine built hospitals and schools, supported religious tolerance, and introduced the Russian nobility to European art, music, architecture, and engineering. But like previous Russian rulers, she did nothing to help the serfs. In 1774, she crushed a peasant rebellion in European Russia and extended serfdom. Her policies gave the nation's landowners more power and widened the gap between rich and poor.

Catherine the Great was the daughter of a German prince. As a teenager, she moved to Russia to marry a grandson of Peter the Great. She became czarina at age thirty-three.

Russia's booming development drew the attention of French emperor Napoléon Bonaparte. After conquering much of western Europe, Napoléon invaded Russia in 1812 with more than six hundred thousand troops. He captured Moscow in September, but as he waited for Czar Alexander I to surrender, the brutal Russian winter set in. Short on supplies and food, the French retreated across the windy, snow-covered plains. Only around twenty to thirty thousand French soldiers survived the ill-fated invasion.

Napoléon Bonaparte's huge army reached Moscow in September 1812. The tide of the war soon turned, and the French were forced to retreat.

In December 1825, a group of Russian rebels called the Decembrists staged an uprising to end the rule of the czars and establish a more democratic form of government. Czar Nicholas I's armed guards quickly put down the revolt, but the Decembrists had shown that the time had come for economic reform in Russia.

When Alexander II came to power in 1855, he began policies to solve his country's problems. He improved the legal and educational systems for all classes. In 1861, he abolished serfdom, freeing about twenty-three million serfs. In return, however, the serfs had to pay their

Peasant women carrying wood on their backs. Peasants had a difficult life, even after serfdom ended.

former landlords for their freedom and land within fifty years. Not many of the peasants could afford these redemption payments, as they were known, and so their lives did not greatly improve. These changes angered landowners, meanwhile, because they depended on the cheap labor provided by the serfs.

Alexander II's reforms failed to heal his country's wounds. In 1881, members of a terrorist organization known as the People's Will assassinated Alexander II in St. Petersburg. His son, Alexander III, took the throne and immediately imposed limits on individual rights and the rights of the press and local governments. He expanded a secret police force and gave landowners more power, further angering the poor.

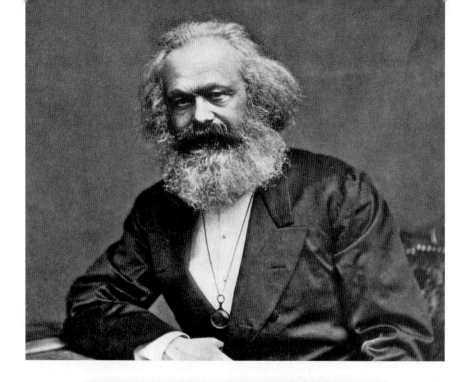

German philosopher Karl Marx explained his ideas about society in the books *The Communist Manifesto* and *Capital.*

The Last Czar

When Alexander III died in 1894, his son, Nicholas II, took the throne. Russia was in turmoil. Anti-czarist feelings were growing, and radical groups opposed to the government began to form. One group, the Marxists, consisted of followers of Karl Marx, a German philosopher and revolutionary. Marx believed that history was determined by the economic struggle between the rich and the poor. He argued that as a result of this battle between bosses and workers, the workers would eventually take control of the government. They would create an ideal state in which everyone was equal. Marxists formed the Russian Social Democratic Labor Party, which later split into two groups, the Bolsheviks and the Mensheviks.

Meanwhile, in 1904, Nicholas II had gotten Russia involved in a disastrous war with Japan in Manchuria, in northeastern China. Russia suffered a terrible defeat. The loss, in addition to widespread poverty and high taxes, created a dangerous political situation that came to a head in January 1905.

Two hundred thousand workers and their families marched to the czar's Winter Palace in St. Petersburg to present a petition to demand reforms. The czar's guards fired on the peace-

Injured Russians lie in the snow on Bloody Sunday.

ful crowd, killing or wounding hundreds of protesters. This massacre, known as Bloody Sunday, triggered hundreds of riots and strikes throughout Russia. Fearing full-scale revolution, Nicholas II approved a constitution that provided for limited democratic reforms, including the establishment of a legislature called the Duma. He also abolished peasant land redemption payments. Because of this, the peasants were no longer in debt, so they could buy larger plots of land to farm.

The World Goes to War

Russia entered World War I in 1914 as an ally of Great Britain and France in their struggle against Germany and Austria. But Russia's army was unprepared for war. Despite some early

Expansion of the Russian Empire

Russia, 1505

Russian Empire, 1598

Acquisitions by 1689

Acquisitions by 1725

Acquisitions by 1796

Acquisitions by 1855

Acquisitions by 1914

19th- to 20th-century
sphere of influence

Present-day Russia

victories, many Russian soldiers were wounded or killed. Shortages of food and supplies on the battlefield and at home made the situation worse. To support the war, taxes were increased, placing an even greater strain on the poverty-stricken Russian people. Despair was at an all-time high.

Revolution

During this troubled time, the royal family's problems deepened with the arrival of Grigory Rasputin. He was a peasant mystic who claimed to have magical healing powers. Rasputin convinced Nicholas's wife, Empress Alexandra, that he could

Holy Man or Mad Man?

During the reign of Czar Nicholas II, a mysterious figure appeared in St. Petersburg. His name was Grigory Rasputin (1872–1916), and he had been born in western Siberia. After spending time in a monastery and claiming he had a vision of Mary, the mother of Jesus, he became a wanderer and religious mystic. He arrived in St. Petersburg in 1903 and gained the reputation of being able to heal the sick.

Empress Alexandra summoned Rasputin to the royal court to cure her son. Seemingly successful, Alexandra came to believe that God spoke to her through Rasputin. Rasputin won the trust of Nicholas and Alexandra and began to exert control over the royal family.

Eventually, Rasputin became unpopular in Russia. He was accused of being a fraud whose influence over the royal family posed great danger to the country. Many people called him the Mad Monk.

On a wintry night in December 1916, a group of nobles who wanted to end Rasputin's control over the royal family invited him to dinner. They poisoned his food, but he was unaffected. One of the princes then shot him, but that too failed to kill the Mad Monk. Rasputin repeatedly lunged at his assassins, and was shot again and again. While he was still alive, the nobles wrapped him in a carpet and threw him into the icy Neva River, where he finally perished.

Rasputin's death opened the door for revolutionaries and others who opposed czarist rule to seize control of the nation.

heal her son, Alexis, of hemophilia, a deadly blood disease. Rasputin gained power over Nicholas through his influence on the czarina. He influenced many political decisions. Nobles and peasants thought Rasputin was a threat to the nation and the royal family, and in 1916, a group of aristocrats killed him.

In February 1917, protesters rioted in St. Petersburg. Rather than shoot the rioters, the royal guard turned their guns on the officers and joined the rebels. Nicholas was forced to give up his throne.

The Duma quickly formed a new government. To influence the decisions of the government, workers formed councils called soviets. Reform was slow to come, and some soviets demanded immediate action. They wanted to end the war with Germany, and they wanted peasants to seize control of land and factories.

After the failed revolution of 1905, Bolshevik leader Vladimir Ilyich Lenin had fled to western Europe. While in exile, he supervised the activities of the Bolsheviks in Russia. In April 1917, he secretly returned to St. Petersburg to stir up a revolution. The government put down his demonstrations, and Lenin fled to Finland. He returned several months later to lead a revolution that would change history.

The night of November 6, 1917, was the start of the Russian Revolution, also called the October Revolution. (According to the calendar that Russia used at the time, the revolution began in October.) Led by Lenin, the Bolsheviks seized power and established the Russian Soviet Federative Socialist Republic, based on the principles of Marxism.

Leader of the Revolution

Vladimir Ilyich Lenin (1870–1924) was one of the most influential thinkers and political figures of the twentieth century. He founded the Russian Communist Party, masterminded the Bolshevik takeover of Russia, and was the first leader of the USSR.

Lenin was born in Simbirsk, about 400 miles (645 km) east of Moscow, into a well-educated family (Lenin as a child, below, front right). He studied law at Kazan University, where he was exposed to the thinking of Karl Marx. Lenin was expelled from school for his radical policies, but continued his studies independently and earned his law degree.

He moved to St. Petersburg, where he spread his revolutionary ideas. In 1897, he was exiled to Siberia for plotting against Alexander III. At the end of his exile in 1900, he moved to Europe where he spent the next fifteen years. There he became a major figure in the international revolutionary movement and the leader

of the Bolshevik wing of the Russian Social Democratic Labor Party.

In 1917, he secretly returned to Russia. Lenin led the Bolsheviks' October Revolution. After three years of civil war, Lenin and the Bolsheviks gained total control of the nation.

Lenin died in 1924. His body was preserved in a glass coffin in a tomb in Moscow's Red Square, where it still lies today. Visitors stand in line to get a chance to see his body.

Starving Russians gather around a train where food is being distributed during the famine of 1921.

Lenin moved Russia's capital back to Moscow, renamed his political group the Communist Party, and pulled Russia out of World War I. In the summer of 1918, he ordered the execution of the royal family, who had been under arrest since the October Revolution. Lenin's government seized lands owned by nobles, the church, and the peasants. It took control of the banks and began controlling the sales and distribution of food and the most basic goods. Lenin also established the Cheka, a secret police, to deal with people suspected of treason.

When a drought from 1920 to 1921 resulted in a famine that killed as many as five million people, Lenin responded with his New Economic Policy. Some businesses and factories were returned to private control and farmers were permitted to sell their crops and keep a portion of their harvests.

Lenin expanded Communism into the nearby republics of Belarus, Ukraine, Georgia, Azerbaijan, and Armenia. In December 1922, he brought them into the nation, forming the Union of Soviet Socialist Republics, or USSR.

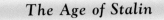

The Age of Stalin

After Lenin died in 1924, two men vied for power: Joseph Stalin, the head of the Communist Party, and Leon Trotsky, a more radical Communist. Stalin won the bitter struggle, and he had Trotsky exiled and then murdered.

The Russian economy had been devastated by war and revolution. To help revive it, Stalin instituted the first of his Five-Year Plans in 1929. The state established production goals that industry and agriculture had to meet. To increase crop production to feed the nation, he made farmers pool their land in collective farms. Farmers were forced to hand over their harvests to the state to meet the new production goals.

Joseph Stalin was a brutal leader who persecuted anyone who opposed him. Millions of people were killed during his regime.

Workers stand atop an iron and steel factory in Magnitogorsk. The city, which sits on a huge vein of iron, grew rapidly in the 1930s under the Five-Year Plans.

The Five-Year Plans virtually eliminated private business, denying people the chance to profit from their own work. Although Russia had grown into a huge industrial power, industry and agriculture were unable to meet Stalin's unrealistic goals. Between 1932 and 1933, a devastating famine struck the USSR,

hitting Ukraine and Kazakhstan particularly hard. Roughly six million people died, and a new period of unrest began.

Stalin responded by imprisoning and killing millions of people he suspected of being disloyal or unsupportive of his policies. This period is called the Great Terror. No one was safe: politicians, labor leaders, and even workers were brutally punished by the state.

World War II

In the 1930s, Germany, led by Adolf Hitler, dramatically increased its military power and seized land in central and eastern Europe. To protect itself from German aggression, Stalin signed a nonaggression treaty with Hitler in 1939. The two nations agreed to invade and divide Poland. Stalin also took control of Latvia, Lithuania, and Estonia.

But Hitler betrayed Stalin. In June 1941, two years after the start of World War II, Germany invaded the Soviet Union. Stalin immediately began to fight against Germany on the side of the Allied nations Great Britain and France. The United States joined the Allies in December 1941. After more than two years of bitter fighting on Soviet soil, the German army was defeated. The fighting spirit of the Russian people, combined with the harsh Russian winter, helped drive the German army from Russia.

The war ended in 1945. It had devastated Russia. More than twenty-five million Soviet soldiers and civilians had been killed, and millions of others were injured or missing. Nearly one hundred thousand towns, cities, and villages had been wiped out. Farms were in ruins and factories had been leveled.

The Cold War

After the war ended, the victorious Allied nations divided up Europe. The United States, Great Britain, and France took control of western Germany. The Soviet Union occupied eastern Germany, Poland, Czechoslovakia, Bulgaria, Albania, Romania, and Hungary. The Soviets installed Communist dictators as leaders of these countries, called satellite states, and crushed all democratic opposition. As the Soviets exerted control over all of Eastern Europe, Britain's prime minister, Winston Churchill, declared that an "Iron Curtain" had fallen between Eastern and Western Europe. On one side were lands dominated by the Soviet Union; on the other side were the independent countries of Western Europe.

The Soviet Union kept tight control of its satellite states. After Czechoslovakia began allowing its people more freedom in the late 1960s, the Soviets sent tanks and troops into the nation to stop the changes.

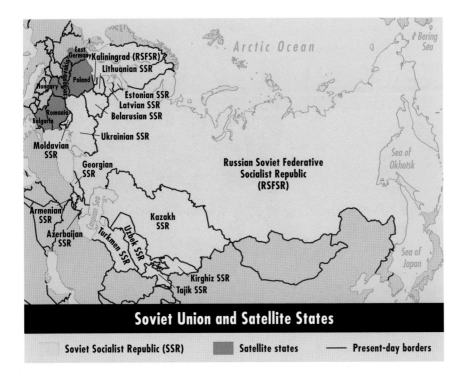

Soviet Union and Satellite States

Soviet Socialist Republic (SSR)   Satellite states   —— Present-day borders

At the same time, tensions were growing between the United States and the Soviet Union. This became known as the Cold War. The United States and other Western nations feared that the Soviet Union would spread Communism around the globe. In 1949, the Soviets built their first nuclear bomb. The rivalry between the United States and the USSR intensified as the two nations engaged in an arms race for military superiority. The world feared that a devastating nuclear war could occur at any time.

In the 1950s, the Cold War competition extended into space exploration. Nikita Khrushchev, the leader of the Soviet Union, engaged the United States in a "space race." The Soviets sent *Sputnik 1*, the world's first satellite, into orbit in 1957. The Soviets also won the race to send the first human into space. In 1961, cosmonaut (Russian astronaut) Yuri

First into Space

Until 1968, the town of Gagarin in far western Russia was known as Gzhatsk. In that year, the town was renamed in honor of Yuri Gagarin, Russia's first cosmonaut, the Russian term for "astronaut."

Gagarin was born in 1934 in the nearby village of Klushino. As a youngster, he became interested in space and astronomy. He entered military flight training in 1955 and became a lieutenant in the Soviet air force two years later. In 1960, he was selected for the Soviet space program and entered the training program from which the first cosmonauts were selected.

On April 12, 1961, Gagarin was sent into outer space aboard the *Vostok 1* spacecraft, becoming the first human to travel into space and the first to orbit Earth. His total time in space was 1 hour and 48

minutes. After his flight, Gagarin became a worldwide celebrity and visited many countries to promote the Soviet space program. He died in a plane crash in March 1968 during a routine training flight.

Gagarin became the first person to orbit Earth, a year before the first American astronaut did the same.

In 1964, Leonid Brezhnev (1906–1982) came to power. He created a policy that would send Soviet troops into nearby nations if the nations seemed unstable. Brezhnev sent troops to Czechoslovakia in 1968 and to Afghanistan in 1979. The war in Afghanistan lasted nine years and drained the Soviet economy. The cost of the war added to the country's inability to produce enough food or goods for the people.

The Cold War Thaws

Mikhail Gorbachev came to power in 1985 determined to reshape the Soviet Union. He introduced the policies of *glas-*

The Cuban Missile Crisis

In October 1962, a U.S. spy plane photographed nuclear missile sites being built by the Soviet Union on Cuba in the Caribbean Sea. Cuba, a Communist nation, lies only 90 miles (145 km) from the coast of southern Florida. The missiles were in striking distance of major U.S. cities. U.S. president John F. Kennedy ordered a naval blockade of Cuba to prevent more Soviet Union military supplies from reaching the island. Kennedy then demanded that the Soviets remove the missiles and destroy the sites.

Kennedy went on national television to explain the crisis to the American people. Thirteen tense days passed as the world waited to see how Soviet leader Nikita Khrushchev would respond to the U.S. demands. Recognizing America's military superiority in the skies and seas around Cuba, Khrushchev finally agreed to Kennedy's terms in return for a public U.S. promise to not invade Cuba. More than twenty-five years later, it was revealed that the United States also promised to remove its nuclear missiles from Turkey, which is located near Russia.

Although worldwide nuclear devastation was avoided, the Cuban missile crisis did not end the arms race. Both the United States and the Soviet Union continued ramping up their missile supplies for many more years.

nost ("openness") and *perestroika* ("restructuring") to improve the economy and reform the government. Gorbachev encouraged Russians to voice their opinions about the government and to work together with it to find solutions. He released political prisoners and made agreements with the United States to decrease the number of nuclear weapons. He also held free national elections—the first in Russia since 1917.

A Voice for Freedom

Yelena Bonner (1923–2011) was a noted human rights activist in the Soviet Union. Bonner was born in the region that is present-day Turkmenistan, a former republic of the Soviet Union. Her father was executed during the Great Terror, and her mother was arrested and sent to a forced labor camp.

During the 1940s, Bonner began aiding political prisoners and their families. Although a member of the Communist Party, she became more active in the Soviet human rights movement in the 1960s. Swept up in the anti-Communist movement, she quit the party. In 1972, she married physicist and political activist Andrei D. Sakharov (far right), who was critical of the Communist regime. In 1975, Sakharov was awarded the Nobel Peace Prize.

In 1976, Bonner helped found the Moscow Helsinki Group, an organization that monitored human rights violations in the Soviet Union. In 1984, she was exiled

to Siberia on charges of anti-Soviet activities. There, she joined her husband who had been exiled four years earlier for speaking out against the Soviet invasion of Afghanistan.

In 1986, Soviet leader Mikhail Gorbachev freed the couple from exile and requested that they return to the USSR. At that time, Gorbachev was beginning to push his reforms and policy of *glasnost*. Sakharov and Bonner agreed, but they both continued their fight for human rights. In the 1990s, Bonner was highly critical of Vladimir Putin's leadership, accusing him of reverting to old-style dictatorial Communist policies. She continued to be an outspoken supporter of human rights and democracy throughout the world until her death in 2011.

As the government gave up control of the economy, prices soared, and goods and services became costly and difficult to obtain. The Communist Party weakened, and Soviet states in Eastern Europe overthrew their Communist regimes.

At the end of 1991, the Soviet Union crumbled. The USSR was replaced by a group of independent republics, including Russia, which is formally known as the Russian Federation.

The Russian Federation

The transition from the old system to a more democratic government and noncommunist economy was not easy. Boris Yeltsin

Red Square

Red Square in Moscow is the heart and soul of Russia: it is the embodiment of the nation's turbulent and complex past. The square's name does not come from the color of the brick streets and buildings or because red is the color associated with Communism. Its name comes from the Russian word *krasnaya*, which means both "beautiful" and "red." The name Red Square dates back to the seventeenth century.

Red Square was originally the primary marketplace and trade center in Moscow. Russia's first department store was built there at the end of the nineteenth century. In the Soviet era, Red Square became the nation's most important site. The Kremlin, the seat of the Soviet government, was located on the square. Military parades were often held there, with thousands of troops, tanks, missiles, and other weapons showcasing the nation's military might.

Many buildings on the square capture the history and spirit of the Russian people. Lenin's Mausoleum contains the body of Vladimir Lenin. Nearby is St. Basil's Cathedral, a Russian Orthodox church built by Ivan the Terrible in the 1500s. The swirling, onion-shaped domes of green, red, and orange have become a symbol of Russia.

Chechen fighters stand on a captured Russian tank during the 1994 rebellion in Grozny, the capital of Chechnya.

was the first president of the Russian Federation. He tried to reform the economy, but the Russian standard of living was failing and people grew angry. Responding to harsh opposition, he dismissed the Duma in 1993. When many lawmakers refused to leave the legislative building in Red Square, in the heart of Moscow, Yeltsin ordered tanks to fire on the building. Dozens of people were killed, but Yeltsin remained in power.

In December 1993, the Russian parliament approved a new constitution based largely on the constitutions of democratic Western nations. The constitution also expanded the powers of the Russian president.

In the early 1990s, many people in Chechnya, a region of Russia located in the northern Caucasus Mountains, demanded to become a separate nation. In 1994, during the rebellion, Yeltsin sent in troops to crush the uprising. He was not able to completely defeat the rebels, and the violence continues on and off to this day.

The Twenty-First Century

Toward the end Yeltsin's time in office, he named Vladimir V. Putin prime minister. When Yeltsin later resigned, he named Putin acting president, placing Putin in good standing for the presidential election of 2000, which he easily won. As president, Putin called for a stronger central government and for free-market economic reforms. Putin was accused of undemocratic policies such as trying to exert control over the Russian media and Russia's oil industries. Under his leadership, however, Putin brought stability and economic progress, making him popular with Russian voters.

In March 2008, Dmitry Medvedev was elected president and he named Putin prime minister again. Medvedev continued many of Putin's policies, and in 2012, Putin was once again elected president.

Vladimir Putin (far left) and Dmitry Medvedev walk to a meeting.

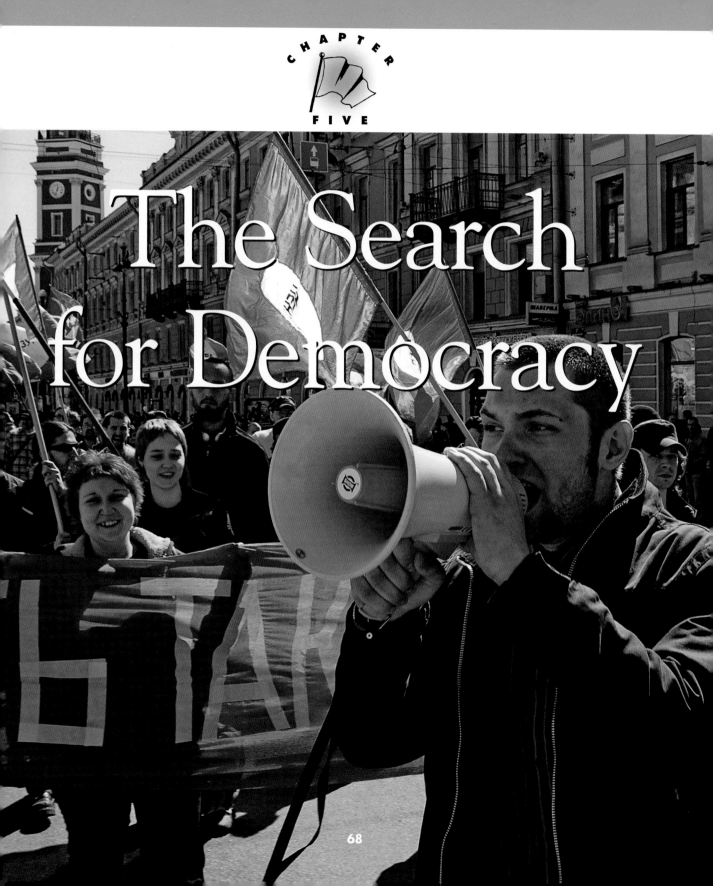

The Search
for Democracy

R USSIA IS A FEDERATION AND A REPUBLIC. A federation is a nation made up of partially self-governing states. A republic is a form of government in which ultimate power rests with the people, through their ability to vote. As in the United States and Canada, the Russian government is made up of three branches: executive, legislative, and judiciary.

Opposite: **Members of the Communist Party protest against the government. Russians have more freedom than they had in the past, and protests are now allowed.**

The Executive Branch

The executive branch includes the president and prime minister. The president is the head of state, and the prime minister is the head of government. Russia's president is elected by the people for a six-year term and can serve two consecutive terms. The Russian constitution adopted in 1993 gave the president far-reaching powers in establishing domestic and foreign policy and overseeing the nation's security and defense. The president can issue decrees, which are laws that do not have to be passed by the Duma, and may even dissolve the legislature in times of emergency. The president also appteints the prime minister, cabinet ministers, and members of the judicial branch, with the approval of the Duma.

The prime minister is responsible for the daily operations of the government. He or she enforces the constitution, federal laws, and presidential decrees. The prime minister also recommends to the president people to serve as department and agency ministers. Together with the other ministers, the prime minister prepares the government budget, which must be approved by the Federal Assembly. If the president dies or

President Dmitry Medvedev attends a meeting with cabinet members. In 2012, the Russian government included a prime minister, seven deputy prime ministers, and twenty-one other ministers.

Powerful Leader

Vladimir Putin has been either the prime minister or president of Russia since 1999. Putin was born in 1952 in Leningrad, now St. Petersburg. His father was in the navy, and his mother worked in a factory. Putin studied law and joined the KGB, the Russian secret police, after finishing college.

After the Soviet Union fell apart in 1991, Putin became involved in politics. He rose to become an important aide to President Boris Yeltsin. In 1999, Yeltsin made him prime minister, and when Yeltsin resigned, he took over the presidency.

Putin's presidency had both positive and negative aspects. On the positive side, the Russian economy grew during Putin's time in power. On the negative side, Putin increased the power of the government and refused to tolerate opposing voices. Many people criticized him for limiting the power of the press. He is considered by some people to be an enemy of democracy.

In May 2012, Putin was sworn in once again as president of the Russian Federation.

leaves office unexpectedly, the prime minister becomes the president until new elections take place.

The Legislative Branch

The legislative branch is Russia's lawmaking parliament called the Federal Assembly. The Federal Assembly includes two bodies, the Federation Council and the Duma. The Federation Council has 166 members. They represent all 83 administrative sectors, or subjects, within the Russian Federation. Two members are chosen from each subject. The local legislature

The Flag

Russia's flag has three horizontal stripes: white, blue, and red. Created in 1697, it was originally the banner for Russian merchant ships and warships. It became the official state flag in 1896 and was used until 1917, when the Bolsheviks seized control of the government. Following the collapse of the Soviet Union in 1991, the tricolor flag was put into use again.

elects one member, and the local governor elects the other. The Federation Council approves treaties, considers use of Russia's armed forces outside the Russian Federation, and reviews tax and budget bills. It also approves nominations to the national courts.

Newly elected members attend the opening session of the Duma in 2011.

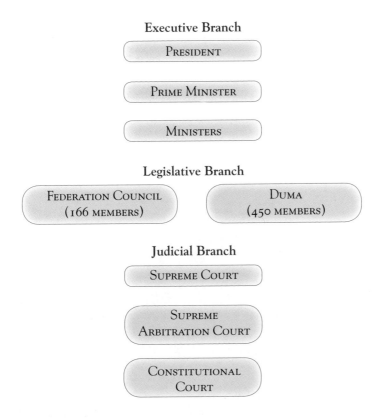

National Government of Russia

Executive Branch

PRESIDENT

PRIME MINISTER

MINISTERS

Legislative Branch

FEDERATION COUNCIL
(166 MEMBERS)

DUMA
(450 MEMBERS)

Judicial Branch

SUPREME COURT

SUPREME
ARBITRATION COURT

CONSTITUTIONAL
COURT

The Duma has 450 deputies, each elected to a five-year term by a system of proportional representation. In this system, each party is given a number of seats in proportion to the number of votes it receives. The Duma approves spending and operating expenses for the government and works with the Federation Council to make laws.

The Judicial Branch

The Supreme Court is Russia's highest court. Its twenty-three members hear civil, criminal, and administrative cases. The

Russia's National Anthem

The music of "Gosudarstvenny Gimn Rossiyskoy Federatsii" ("National Anthem of the Russian Federation"), the nation's national anthem, was also the music of the national anthem of the Soviet Union. Alexander Alexandrov composed it around 1939. After the breakup of the Soviet Union, a contest was held to find words for the music. Lyrics by children's book author and fabulist Sergey Mikhalkov were selected in 2000, and the anthem was officially adopted in December of that year.

Russia—our holy nation,
Russia—our beloved country.
A mighty will, great glory—
Yours given for all time!

Be glorious, our free Fatherland,
Age-old union of fraternal peoples,
National wisdom given by our forebears!
Be glorious, our country! We are proud of you!

From the southern seas to the polar lands
Spread are our forests and fields.
You are unique in the world, one of a kind—
Native land protected by God!

Wide spaces for dreams and for living
Are opened for us by the coming years.
Our loyalty to our Fatherland gives us strength.
Thus it was, thus it is and always will be!

Supreme Court of Arbitration, which is composed of one chair and four deputy chairs, resolves economic disputes. The Constitutional Court, which has nineteen members, decides whether federal laws, presidential decrees, and local constitutions are constitutional. Judges of the highest courts serve for life.

Political Parties

During the Soviet era, the Communist Party was the only political party allowed in Russia. Today, there are seven registered political parties in the country. The United Russia party is by far the most popular, holding almost 53 percent of the seats in the Duma. The Communist Party still maintains a presence, filling about 20 percent of the Duma's seats. Other important parties include the Liberal Democratic Party and A Just Russia.

Members of the Liberal Democratic Party of Russia prepare pamphlets and other materials. The party holds the fourth-largest number of seats in the Duma.

Russia's Federal Subjects

Russia is composed of eighty-three federal subjects. There are forty-six oblasts (provinces), each with a federally appointed governor and an elected legislature. Each of the twenty-one republics has its own constitution with an elected president or prime minister. The republics are intended to be the homes for specific ethnic minorities and may establish their own language alongside Russian. There are also nine *krais* (territories), four *okrugs* (autonomous districts), one autonomous oblast, and two federal cities (Moscow and St. Petersburg).

A Visit to Moscow

Moscow, Russia's capital and most populous city, is the political, economic, social, and cultural center of the Russian Federation. With a population of 11,514,330, it is the largest city in Europe.

Moscow was founded in 1147. Through the centuries, it served as the capital of medieval Russia and the Soviet Union.

Moscow has warm, humid summers and long, cold winters. The average high temperature in July is 76°F (24°C), but in January the average high is only 25°F (-4°C). Snow is typically on the ground from the end of November until mid-March.

The streets of Moscow are laid out like a wheel, with highways running like spokes from the center of the city. Getting around Moscow is easy by walking or riding buses, trams, or the subway system, called the Moscow Metro. The original Metro stations built between 1932 and 1954 are handsomely decorated with mosaics, stained glass, and ornate chandeliers. The decor of each station depicts a theme that glorifies the Soviet

Union, such as the October Revolution, Russia's military strength, or its industrial accomplishments.

Red Square, with its cathedrals and political buildings, is the heart of Moscow.

Gorky Park, which opened in 1928, is another favorite Moscow attraction. It has play areas, lush flower gardens, and ponds. In the winter, the pathways flood and freeze over, making it possible for visitors to skate around the park.

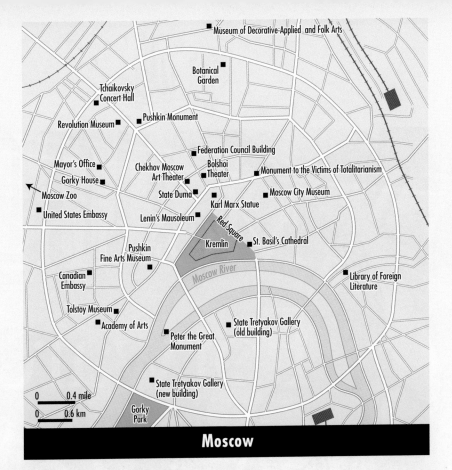

Museum of Decorative-Applied and Folk Arts
Botanical Garden
Tchaikovsky Concert Hall
Pushkin Monument
Revolution Museum
Federation Council Building
Mayor's Office
Chekhov Moscow Art Theater
Bolshoi Theater
Monument to the Victims of Totalitarianism
Gorky House
Moscow Zoo
State Duma
Moscow City Museum
Karl Marx Statue
United States Embassy
Lenin's Mausoleum
Red Square
St. Basil's Cathedral
Pushkin Fine Arts Museum
Kremlin
Canadian Embassy
Moscow River
Library of Foreign Literature
Tolstoy Museum
State Tretyakov Gallery (old building)
Academy of Arts
Peter the Great Monument
State Tretyakov Gallery (new building)
0   0.4 mile
0   0.6 km
Gorky Park

Moscow

CHAPTER SIX

Moving Forward

RUSSIA'S ECONOMY HAS HAD A TROUBLED PAST. For centuries, czars controlled the land and the peasants who farmed it. The workers were little more than slaves, toiling for wealthy landowners or for the government. The industrial boom of the late nineteenth century helped the nation prosper, but the czar and the nobles still controlled the economy. Factory workers received little pay, and peasants usually had little land of their own to farm.

Opposite: **A poster from 1920, shortly after the Bolshevik Revolution, shows Russians hard at work in a factory.**

After the Revolution

The Bolshevik Revolution in 1917 brought dramatic change to the economy. The government took control of private property and planned all phases of business, industry, and agricultural production. It determined what would be grown on farms and produced in factories. It also set prices. Stalin's Five-Year Plans were intended to quickly grow Russia's economy. They helped transform the country into an industrial and military power. The government's command of the economy did not encourage the workers' creativity and initiative, however. This prevented new technologies from being developed.

The collapse of the Soviet Union in 1991 marked yet another era of change. Under Mikhail Gorbachev, the state eased its control on the economy. When the government gave up price controls, however, the cost of food and necessary goods skyrocketed, and unemployment rose. Crime and corruption became widespread as people struggled to survive in the new economy.

By 2001, the economy was showing signs of bouncing back. Between 2000 and 2010, monthly wages rose from $80 per month to $750. In 1998, 40 percent of Russians lived in poverty. By 2010, the number had gone down to 13 percent.

Money Matters

The ruble is the unit of currency in the Russian Federation. Each ruble is divided into one hundred kopeks. The ruble is one of the world's oldest currencies, first appearing in the fifteenth century. In 2011, 31 rubles equaled one U.S. dollar.

Coins come in values of 1, 5, 10, and 50 kopeks. They show St. George slaying a dragon, which has been an important image in the Russian Orthodox Church for centuries. There are also coins worth 1, 2, 5, and 10 rubles, which feature the Russian national symbol of a double-headed eagle. Russia issues paper money in values of 50, 100, 500, 1,000, and 5,000 rubles. The 50-ruble note shows the Old St. Petersburg Stock Exchange with its ornate columns. The 100-ruble note shows a statue of a chariot being pulled by four horses and the Bolshoi Theater in Moscow.

The worldwide economic crisis in 2008 and 2009, however, stopped Russia's booming economy in its tracks. The price of oil, one of Russia's largest exports, dropped drastically. Foreign investments all but dried up. The government spent billions of dollars to reverse the sagging economy, and the situation finally eased at the end of 2009. In 2011, with a $2.2 trillion gross domestic product (GDP)—the total value of all goods and services produced in a country—Russia had the seventh-largest economy in the world.

Gleaming skyscrapers were built in Moscow during the economic boom of the early 2000s.

Services

Since 2000, the service sector—which includes health care, tourism, sales, real estate, banking, and much more—has been the largest part of the Russian economy. Roughly 58 percent of all jobs are in services. With private ownership of businesses

The AvtoVaz factory in Togliatti, in southwestern Russia, is one of the largest auto plants in the world. It produces nearly one million cars a year.

on the rise, new supermarkets, malls, restaurants, and movie theaters have opened. Each new business creates job opportunities for Russians, particularly among the young.

Industry

Industry, which includes manufacturing, energy, and mining, accounts for 32 percent of Russian jobs. These workers produce machinery, food products, automobiles, aircraft, iron and steel, electronics, and communication equipment. The defense industry is the largest employer in the manufacturing sector, providing 20 percent of all manufacturing jobs. Russia is second only to the United States in exporting weapons, which include helicopters, tanks, jet fighters, and air defense systems.

Russia is one of the world's leading producers of oil. In 2010, it produced 10.1 billion gallons per day, ranking second only to Saudi Arabia. The strength of Russia's economy is closely tied to the price of oil. When oil prices drop, Russia cannot pay back money it has borrowed from foreign banks and businesses. This scares off foreign investors. Since 2000, oil prices have skyrocketed, and Russia's economy has strengthened.

Workers repair an oil well in Siberia.

What Russia Grows, Makes, and Mines

Agriculture (2009)

Wheat	61,740,000 metric tons
Milk	32,326,000 metric tons
Potatoes	31,134,000 metric tons

Manufacturing (2007, value added by manufacturing)

Petroleum products	US$36,216,000,000
Iron and steel	US$19,399,000,000
Food products	US$17,159,000,000

Mining (2008)

Nickel	266,807 metric tons
Mica	100,000 metric tons
Platinum metals	123,200 kilograms
Diamonds	21,925,000 karats

Russia's reserves of natural gas stand at 47.5 trillion cubic meters, the largest such reserve in the world. Iran, with the second-largest reserve, has roughly 29.6 million cubic meters in reserves. Russia is also a major producer of coal, with reserves second only to those in the United States.

Russia's mineral-rich landscape includes sizable deposits of iron ore, lead, zinc, nickel, tin, asbestos, gold, and diamonds. Many of these deposits are located in remote regions of Siberia, making them difficult to mine and transport. Few workers are willing to work and live in the harsh Siberian regions.

Agriculture and Fishing

About 10 percent of Russians are employed in agriculture. During the Soviet era, agricultural land in Russia was owned by the state. After 1991, it was privatized, but many problems remain. Most of the land did not end up in the hands of individual farmers. Instead, large corporations manage much of it. Without government supervision, farmers are having difficulty finding markets for their crops. And many farmers are unable to afford new machinery.

A man shovels wheat on a farm near the Black Sea. Russia produces about 10 percent of all the wheat in the world.

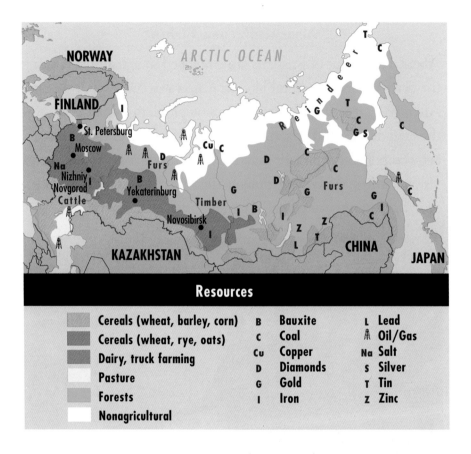

Resources

▨ Cereals (wheat, barley, corn)	B	Bauxite	L	Lead
▨ Cereals (wheat, rye, oats)	C	Coal	⚒	Oil/Gas
▨ Dairy, truck farming	Cu	Copper	Na	Salt
▨ Pasture	D	Diamonds	S	Silver
▨ Forests	G	Gold	T	Tin
▨ Nonagricultural	I	Iron	Z	Zinc

Only 10 percent of the land in Russia is suitable for farming. Most Russian farmland is found in the southwest. Russia's main crops are wheat, barley, oats, corn, sugar beets, sunflowers, fruits, and berries.

Russia's coastline is the third longest in the world. With access to three oceans, the Caspian and Black Seas, and more than two million rivers, fishing is an important industry in the country. In 2009, Russian fishers hauled in 4.3 million tons (3.9 million metric tons) of fish. Important catch includes pollock, herring, whiting, cod, and perch.

Russia has more forestland than any other nation. Forests cover more than 2,470 million acres (1,000 million hectares)—an area larger than the continental United States. The timber industry contributes an estimated $20 billion to the economy each year.

Forestland, like farmland, has been privatized, with much of the land going to private companies. Each year, Russia exports millions of tons of wood pulp products, paper, and cardboard products. Timber is often exported illegally, which harms the economy and forces Russians to buy back their own wood and wood products from other nations.

Logs are piled high in a forest in northern Russia. Russia is the world's largest exporter of logs.

Most of Russia's 63,380 miles (102,000 km) of waterways are natural rivers or lakes. A large system of canals connects major rivers. Canals connect Moscow to the Baltic, White, Caspian, Azov, and Black Seas. The Lenin Volga-Don Canal is one of Russia's most important artificial waterways. It connects two of Russia's major rivers, the Volga and Don. Through this connection, ships can access the Caspian and Azov Seas and the world's oceans. Ships carry roughly 13.4 million tons (12 million metric tons) of cargo on the canal each year.

A barge moves through the Volga-Don Canal.

Major ports in Russia are Kaliningrad and St. Petersburg on the Baltic; Astrakhan and Makhachkala on the Caspian; Petropavlovsk-Kamchatsky and Vladivostok on the Pacific; and Murmansk on the Barents Sea in the Arctic Ocean.

In a country as large as Russia, being able to efficiently move people and goods from place to place is crucial. Russia's vast railway network is second only to that in the United States. There are roughly 54,000 miles (87,000 km) of track covering the nation. The

The Bering Strait Tunnel

Czar Nicholas II dreamed of linking Siberia with North America. This dream is finally becoming a reality. In August 2011, the Russian government approved plans for the construction of a 65-mile-long (105 km) tunnel across the Bering Strait, connecting Siberia and Alaska. The tunnel will be twice as long as the Channel Tunnel that connects England and France, and will cost an estimated $65 billion to build. The tunnel will be part of an anticipated 3,700-mile-long (6,000 km) railroad connecting Yakutsk in Russia with British Columbia in Canada. In addition to the rail tracks, this passageway would also contain pipelines for oil and gas.

The Bering Strait tunnel will boost trade and tourism between Russia and North America, but it is still a long way off. It is estimated that the tunnel and railway system will be completed by 2045.

Trans-Siberian Railway is the world's longest railroad, running 5,772 miles (9,289 km) between Moscow, in Russia's far west, and Vladivostok in the far southeast on the Pacific Ocean. It crosses seven time zones and is the only continuous transportation system through Siberia.

With 610,000 miles (982,000 km) of paved and unpaved roads, Russia ranks eighth in the world in total length of roads. Russia's harsh climate and vast distances make highway construction and maintenance a difficult challenge. Most freight in Russia is carried on the railroad systems.

The Trans-Siberian Railway runs along Lake Baikal. It takes at least six days to ride the full length of the railway from Moscow to Vladivostok.

A Land of Many Faces

THE RUSSIAN FEDERATION IS ONE OF THE MOST ethnically diverse nations in the world. About 80 percent of its people are ethnic Russians. Tatars, the descendants of the Mongols, account for about 4 percent of the population. More than one hundred other ethnic groups live in the Russian Federation. These include Ukrainians and Belarusians in the west; Ossetians and Chechens in the Caucasus Mountains; Turkic peoples in the Volga River region; Yakuts and Samoyeds in Siberia; and Karelians near Russia's border with Finland. Many ethnic groups have established their own republics or independent territories within the Russian Federation.

In 2012, there were about 143 million people in Russia, but since 1997, the Russian population has decreased by five million people. In fact, the country's population has decreased for twenty years in a row, from 1992 to 2012. It's predicted that by 2030, the population will drop to about 127 million people.

Also, many people are moving out of Russia. Since 2001, roughly 1.25 million people have left the country, most often

Opposite: **The Koryak people live in northeastern Russia. Many of them are reindeer herders.**

Who Lives in Russia?

Russians	80%
Tatars	4%
Ukrainians	2%
Bashkirs	1%
Chuvashes	1%
Others	12%

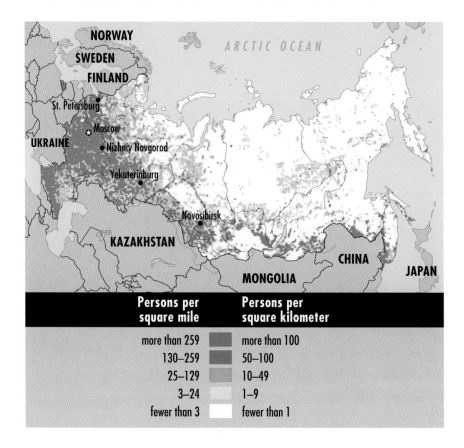

Persons per square mile	Persons per square kilometer
more than 259	more than 100
130–259	50–100
25–129	10–49
3–24	1–9
fewer than 3	fewer than 1

for the United States, England, and Germany. Many of the people leaving are skilled professionals such as teachers, scientists, doctors, and technicians. They are seeking better career opportunities than those available in Russia. Other people are emigrating to get a better education or better medical care, or simply to try a new way of living.

Language

Russian is a branch of the Slavic language family, with roots dating back to the sixth century. The original Slavic language developed into East, West, and South Slavic branches. Russian, Ukrainian, and Belarusian belong to the East branch of the language.

Population of Major Cities (2010 est.)

Moscow	11,514,330
St. Petersburg	4,848,700
Novosibirsk	1,473,737
Yekaterinburg	1,350,136
Nizhniy Novgorod	1,250,615

A Solution to Overcrowding

Moscow's overcrowding and crippling traffic bottlenecks reached an all-time high in 2011. Although the overall population of the country has decreased 1.2 percent since 2002, Moscow's population has grown by two hundred thousand people a year since then. With a current population of 11.5 million people, the capital city has run out of room to grow.

To solve the problem, Russian officials announced that Moscow would expand to the south and southwest, moving into forestland and existing small communities. The expansion will more than double Moscow's current size. Government offices and big businesses will be the first to move to the new areas. Although the government hopes the plan will turn Moscow into an international financial center, many people have voiced strong opposition to the plan. They claim that forestlands will be destroyed and thousands of people will have to be relocated. The government estimates that 250,000 residents will be displaced, but critics believe there will be many more than that. Russian officials estimate it will take twenty years for the project to be completed.

The church books used in Russia following Vladimir I's acceptance of Christianity in 988 were written in Old Church Slavonic. This language got combined with the Slavic language spoken in Kievan Rus and developed into Russian. In later years, Russian absorbed many words from western Europe, especially scientific words and phrases. In the early nineteenth century, writer Aleksandr Pushkin combined traditional words, Old Church Slavic, and western European

The Russian Alphabet

The Russian language uses the Cyrillic alphabet, which was developed in the ninth century by two Greek missionary brothers, St. Cyril and St. Methodius. The brothers created forty-three letters taken from the Greek and Hebrew alphabets to help them translate the Bible from Greek into Slavonic. Modern Russian is closely related to Slavonic. The modern Russian alphabet has thirty-two letters. Other Slavic languages, including Ukrainian, Belarusian, Bulgarian, and Serbian, use different versions of the alphabet.

languages to help create the pronunciations and grammar found in modern Russian.

There are also many non-Slavic languages spoken in Russia, although most people, regardless of their ethnic background, speak Russian as well. Other language groups include Turkic, which is spoken by Tatars and Chuvashes, and Chechen-Ingush, spoken by peoples in the Caucasus.

Common Russian Words and Phrases	
da (DAH)	yes
nyet (nee-ET)	no
zdravstvuite (ZDRAST-voot-yeh)	hello
spasibo (spa-SEE-bah)	thank you
dasvidaniya (das-bee-DAHN-ya)	good-bye
Kak dela? (kak dyi-LAH)	How are you?
Menya zavout . . . (min-YAH za-VOOT) . . .	My name is . . .

Education

In the Soviet era, all Russian citizens were entitled to a free education. Today, Russia ranks among the world's leaders with a literacy rate of more than 99 percent. The state continues to provide free education, although some private institutions have opened and charge tuition fees. Roughly 17 percent of university students pay for their education.

Children are required to attend school for eleven years, starting at age six or seven. Grades 1 to 4 are elementary school, grades 5 to 9 are middle school, and grades 10 to 11 are senior level school. The school year runs from September to May. Typical courses include Russian literature, language,

Only 15 percent of Russians are under age fifteen.

Hard Truths

Although Soviet schools taught Russians how to read and write, the government tightly controlled education. Textbooks praised the ideals of Communism and the Communist Party. They did not, however, report Russia's dark past, particularly the years under Lenin and Stalin. The persecution and murder of millions of Russians by Soviet regimes were simply banished from textbooks. The reforms that came after the collapse of the Soviet Union brought many changes to Russia's education system. In many classrooms, teachers were allowed a choice of textbooks. Students were urged to ask questions and think on their own. Teachers began to encourage open classroom discussions about Russian history, politics, and religion.

and history; mathematics; sciences; foreign languages; art and music; and crafts.

After completing their eleven-year education, Russian students may take the Unified State Examination (USE) if they want to attend a university. More than half of Russians attend university.

Although progress is being made, Russia's uncertain economy has harmed school reform. Many schools are poorly supplied and do not have central heating or running water. Retraining teachers to learn new methods of instruction is very expensive. Teaching has traditionally been a low-paying job, and in recent years teachers have been paid months late. This, combined with the lack of resources and poorly maintained schools, has prompted many teachers to leave their jobs.

From Russian to English

Russian	English	Meaning
bely	beluga	A large fish that lives in the Black Sea or a type of whale
mamot	mammoth	An extinct elephantine hairy animal; something very large or immense
gromit	pogrom	An organized massacre of helpless people
sobol	sable	A weasel-like mammal that lives in northern Asia
samo + varit	samovar	An urn to boil water for tea

Health

Since the collapse of the Soviet Union, the health of the Russian people has declined drastically. The average life expectancy of Russians is 70.3 years, which is eight years less than the U.S. life expectancy. Poor nutrition, alcohol abuse, obesity, smoking, and air and water pollution contribute to Russia's health problems. Russians are the world's heaviest smokers. Seventy percent of men and 40 percent of women between the ages of nineteen and forty-four smoke, and as many as four hundred thousand people die in Russia each year due to smoking-related illnesses. Inadequate medical equipment and facilities and a shortage of well-trained doctors and nurses play a significant role in the poor health of Russians.

Faiths of a
People

RIES, RELIGIOUS PRACTICE
ho rules the country. During
dox Church was the official
other religions were often
he government attempted to
ent seized property from reli-
l believers of all faiths. Many
Atheism, the belief that there
hools. Thousands of churches

iet Union, religion in Russia
dom has increased and more
houses of worship are opening. The Russian Orthodox Church
has regained its importance in Russian culture as the country's
primary religion. Islam is Russia's second-largest religion and
is growing rapidly.

Opposite: **The Trinity Lavra of St. Sergius monastery, located in Sergiyev Posad, northeast of Moscow, is the spiritual center of the Russian Orthodox Church. Its blue-domed Assumption Cathedral was built in the 1500s.**

Religious Affiliation in Russia*

Russian Orthodox	10%–20%
Muslim	10%–15%
Other Christian	2%
Jewish	0.01%

*Includes only practicing worshippers

Russians fill a cathedral in Moscow for a Christmas service.

The Russian Orthodox Church

Christianity was brought to Russia from the Byzantine Empire by Vladimir I in 988. In 1054, when Christianity split into the Eastern (Orthodox) and Western (Roman Catholic) branches, Orthodoxy took hold in Russia. After six hundred years of gradually becoming more and more established, the Orthodox Church became an essential part of the Russian way of life.

Although roughly one hundred million Russian citizens—about 70 percent of the population—consider themselves Orthodox Christians, only about 5 percent attend church on a regular basis.

Orthodox churches are generally built much taller than they are wide, in order to draw the attention of the worshippers upward, to the heavens. At the top of the churches is usually a dome. The inside of the dome is often adorned with an icon of Jesus Christ. An icon is a painting of a religious figure. The walls of a typical Orthodox church are adorned with paintings, icons, and decorative art depicting Christ, saints and prophets, and church festivals.

The high quality and the religious themes of the paintings are meant to inspire worshippers. Beautifully painted icons of saints portrayed in different spiritual states are found in most Orthodox cathedrals. Each figure's face is carefully painted to reflect spirituality. The position of the arms and hands are also important, often gesturing to the heavens.

Other Christian Religions

Several other branches of Christianity are practiced in the Russian Federation. There are roughly 750,000 Roman

Head of the Church

Kirill I, born Vladimir Mikhailovich Gundyayev in Leningrad (now St. Petersburg) in 1946, was elected the Patriarch of the Russian Orthodox Church in 2009. The patriarch is the highest position in the church, similar to the Pope in Roman Catholicism. Kirill has played a key role in the renewal of the church in Russia, in part by developing a good relationship with the Russian government. Kirill is overseeing a rise of religion in Russia. He noted that numerous churches and monasteries throughout Russia have been restored and rebuilt, rejoicing that "the Church has been reborn, and . . . our people [have] been reborn too."

The Kalmyk people are an ethnic group that practices Buddhism. The Kalmyk city of Elista, near the Caspian Sea, is the site of a major Buddhist complex.

Catholics in the country. Many of them are Poles and Lithuanians who settled in Russia. During the Soviet era, many Catholics were persecuted because of their belief in a religion and also because they were not Orthodox.

Protestant churches are also active in Russia. They include Baptists, Lutherans, Pentecostals, Methodists, Quakers, and others. In some parts of Siberia, Protestants outnumber the Russian Orthodox.

Another Christian group, the Jehovah's Witnesses, has grown rapidly. In 1991, there were an estimated 16,000 practitioners in Russia. By 2009, that number had grown to 280,000.

Non-Christian Religions

Islam first appeared in Russia in the eighth century with the Dagestani people. Today, there are roughly 16.5 million Muslims, followers of Islam, living in the Russian Federation. Islam is practiced mainly by the Tatars and Bashkirs of the Volga River basin region, and by the Chechens, Balkars, Kabardin, Dagestani, and other groups of the North Caucasus.

Buddhism appeared in Russia in the early seventeenth century. Tibetan Buddhism is the main form of the religion practiced in Russia today. Followers of Buddhism live mostly in regions near Mongolia.

Followers of Judaism were often persecuted during the reign of the czars and during the Soviet era. In the early twentieth century, roughly half of all Jews in the world lived in Russia. But a series of government-organized massacres called pogroms prompted millions of Jews to flee Russia. In 1990, about one million Jews still lived in the country. In the following years, laws were changed to make it easier for Jews to leave. Hundreds of thousands left Russia for the United States, Israel, Germany, and elsewhere. Today, only about 205,000 Jews remain in Russia.

Grand Choral Synagogue

Built between 1880 and 1888, the Grand Choral Synagogue in St. Petersburg is the second-largest Jewish house of worship in Europe. In 1869, Czar Alexander II granted a permit for Grand Choral to be built, but he placed several restrictions on its construction. It was not allowed to be built near Christian churches or roads used by Russia's czars.

The final design of the synagogue included a swirling dome and detailing done in elegant terra-cotta, a clay-based, unglazed ceramic. During World War I, a hospital was organized on the property to care for wounded soldiers of all faiths. The synagogue was bombed by Germany during World War II, but the damage to the building was not significant.

In the decades after the war, the synagogue fell into disrepair, partly due to the restrictions placed on the practice of Judaism by the Soviet government. But the synagogue underwent a massive restoration between 2000 and 2005 to restore it to its previous beauty. Today, it serves as the center of the Jewish community in St. Petersburg.

A Diverse Culture

RUSSIAN CULTURE BOASTS CENTURIES OF BEAUTY and creativity. During medieval times, the Russian Orthodox Church influenced most of Russia's art and architecture. In the seventeenth century, Russia looked to Europe for cultural inspiration. Czars and wealthy noblemen were the only people who could afford to pay for art, music composition, and building construction. Many of the architects, painters, composers, and craftspeople they hired came from Europe, particularly Italy, Germany, and France.

During the Soviet era, the government supported the fine arts, including ballet, music, painting, and sculpting. The works, however, had to conform to Communist philosophies. The government often banned books and movies that it thought promoted anti-Communist feelings.

Today, there is a reawakening of Russia's rich cultural traditions. Russians now experience and enjoy countless art forms that express the history and culture of their land and people.

Opposite: **Members of the Beryozka folk dance troupe perform a traditional Russian dance.**

Balalaikas come in many sizes. The contrabass balalaika (above) is the largest.

Music

Folk music was Russia's earliest form of musical expression. Common instruments in Russian folk music are the triangular-shaped, three-stringed *balalaika*, the *bayan* accordion, and the *zhaleika*, a flutelike wind instrument.

Folk music influenced many Russian classical composers, including Mikhail Glinka (1804–1857) and Pyotr Tchaikovsky (1840–1893). Glinka is regarded as the father of Russian classical music, and he was the first Russian composer to achieve widespread fame in his own country. He wrote the music for one of Russia's early national anthems. Tchaikovsky is one of the world's greatest composers, whose ballets *The Sleeping*

Beauty, *Swan Lake*, and *The Nutcracker* are still being performed today. He composed the 1812 Overture to celebrate Russia's defense of Moscow against Napoléon's troops. This rousing composition continues to thrill music lovers with the sounds of booming cannon fire and loud clanging bells.

Other important nineteenth-century composers include Modest Petrovich Mussorgsky (1839–1881) and Nikolay Rimsky-Korsakov (1844–1908). Each tried to establish a Russian nationalistic style of classical music. Many of Mussorgsky's works were influenced by Russian history and folklore. He is renowned for compositions such as *Boris Godunov*, *Night on Bald Mountain*, and the piano suite *Pictures*

Swan Lake tells the story of an evil magician who turns a princess into a swan.

at an Exhibition. Rimsky-Korsakov, often finding inspiration in fairy tales, composed the classic *Scheherazade*.

Igor Stravinksy (1882–1971) was one of the world's most influential twentieth-century composers. He is known for his diverse styles and groundbreaking modern pieces. Stravinsky's ballet *The Rite of Spring* caused a riot when it was performed for the first time, in 1913. The unsettling, rhythmic music and violent dance steps prompted booing from the audience. There were arguments, shouting, and, ultimately, fistfights in the aisles of the theater.

Igor Stravinsky was an experimental composer. His works often changed rhythms and had unusual harmonies.

Ballet

Many people consider Russian ballet the best in the world. The Bolshoi Ballet in Moscow and the Mariinsky Ballet in St. Petersburg are both world renowned. In the early twentieth century, Sergey Diaghilev (1872–1929) organized tours of the ballet company he founded, the Ballets Russes. These highly successful tours featured Anna Pavlova (1881–1931) and Vaslav Nijinsky (1890–1950), two of the most famous ballet dancers in history.

Rudolf Nureyev (1938–1993) and Mikhail Baryshnikov (1948–) were the leading male ballet dancers in the mid-twentieth century. Both fled the USSR for the West to pursue their careers.

Mikhail Baryshnikov is renowned for having been an elegant dancer with great leaping ability.

This icon depicting St. Michael the Archangel was painted around the year 1300.

Art

Icons were the main visual art in Russia until the eighteenth century. Most icons are painted on small pieces of wood and displayed in churches or carried through the streets during religious ceremonies. Many people also have icons at home. European-style portrait painting replaced icon painting. Only the wealthy could afford to pay an artist to paint portraits, so the only portraits done were of nobles and their families. Since the collapse of the Soviet Union, icon painting has experienced a national revival.

Ivan Kramskoy (1837–1887) was a painter who became disillusioned with the conservative attitudes of traditional Russian art. He formed a group of young artists who wanted their work to portray the realities of Russian life and historic events. This group was called the *Peredvizhniki* ("wanderers"). One of the Peredvizhniki, Vasily Perov (1834–1882), depicted slices of Russian life in his paintings. Some of the scenes he painted were of peasant parents visiting the grave of their child, a peasant boy sleeping on a curb, and early Christians praying in Kiev.

In the early twentieth century, Russian artists spearheaded the development of several new modern art movements. One of these was suprematism, a type of abstract art. Kazimir Malevich (1878–1935) originated this bold form, which incorporated geometric shapes into dynamic arrangements. His paintings titled *Black Square* and *Black Circle* are simply black shapes painted on white backgrounds.

The new Communist regime originally supported such abstract forms of art. Eventually, however, the state created its own style of art and design called socialist realism. The government commissioned bold, striking images of political leaders, the Soviet military, and proud, happy workers and

Kazimir Malevich founded an art movement called suprematism, based on simple geometric forms. He made this painting, titled *Suprematist Composition*, in 1915.

peasants. Enormous posters of the art were often displayed in towns and cities.

Marc Chagall (1887–1985), one of the twentieth century's greatest painters, left the Soviet Union after Communist authorities imposed socialist realism as the official art style. Chagall's dreamy depictions of Russian peasant life had no place in the Soviet Union, and he spent most of his life in exile, mainly in France.

Marc Chagall in his studio. Chagall was renowned for his expressive use of color.

A World-Class Art Museum

Art lovers from around the world flock to the State Tretyakov Gallery in Moscow, one of Russia's leading museums of fine art. The gallery's collection consists solely of Russian art and works by Russian artists. More than 160,000 works of painting, sculpture, and graphics are on display, ranging from the eleventh to twentieth centuries. The gallery started in 1856 when Russian merchant Pavel Tretyakov began to acquire works by Russian artists of the time. His collection became widely known, and in 1892, he presented it to the Russian nation as a gift.

The collection includes iconic religious paintings such as the twelfth-century *Our Lady of Vladimir* and Andrey Rublyov's fifteenth-century *Holy Trinity*. Modern works are represented by the twentieth-century abstracts *Composition VII* by Wassily Kandinsky, *Black Square* by Kazimir Malevich, and *Over the City* by Marc Chagall.

Literature

Russia produced its greatest works of literature during the nineteenth century. Aleksandr Pushkin (1799–1837) is considered to be Russia's greatest poet and the father of modern Russian literature. He is best known for his novel in verse, *Eugene Onegin*, a tragic tale of love and death. His other important works include *Boris Godunov*, a play about an early Russian ruler, and *The Tales of the Late Ivan Petrovich Belkin*, a series of short stories about a mysterious man.

Nikolay Gogol (1809–1852) made fun of Russia's czarist

monarchies, criticizing their greed and corruption. *Dead Souls*, *The Inspector-General*, and *The Overcoat* are his major works.

In the second half of the nineteenth century, Russian writers made the lives of both the poor and the nobility a frequent theme in their works. Fyodor Dostoyevsky (1821–1881) exposed the true nature of Russian peasant life in great novels such as *Crime and Punishment* and *The Brothers Karamazov*.

Anton Chekhov (1860–1904) was a master writer of short stories and plays. The subjects of his works were often people who felt disconnected from the world and themselves. Chekhov was a brilliant observer of human nature. He was able to capture the lives of both the rich and the poor. His best-known plays are *Uncle Vanya*, *The Cherry Orchard*, *The Three Sisters*, and *The Seagull*.

Leo Tolstoy

Leo Tolstoy (1828-1910), one of the world's greatest novelists, wrote powerful books about the plight of the common man. In *War and Peace* and *Anna Karenina*, Tolstoy examined how character flaws led to tragic lives in nineteenth-century Russia. *War and Peace*, considered by many to be the greatest novel ever written, is a sweeping tale of several families set against the background of Napoléon's invasion of Russia in 1812. Abandoning the riches of his success, Tolstoy searched for spirituality, eventually working with peasants, plowing, and making boots. He became a highly respected thinker on morality and society. His theory of nonviolent resistance to oppressive governments was influential around the world.

Several major Russian writers were victims of government persecution during the Soviet era. Boris Pasternak (1890–1960), who won the Nobel Prize in literature in 1958, is best remembered for his epic novel *Dr. Zhivago*. The novel takes place during the final years of Romanov rule and the beginning of Soviet regimes in Russia. The book was banned in the USSR, but was published in Europe in 1957. When Pasternak won the Nobel Prize the following year, the Communist Party was furious and forced him to turn down the prize.

Aleksandr Solzhenitsyn (1918–2008) is best known for *The Gulag Archipelago* and *One Day in the Life of Ivan Denisovich*. Both novels describe the horrors of life in the Gulag, the Soviet Union's forced labor camp system located in Siberia and the Russian Far East. Enraged authorities threw Solzhenitsyn out of the USSR, but he returned in 1994 after the collapse of the Soviet Union.

Aleksandr Solzhenitsyn was arrested in 1945 for criticizing the government and was kept in prisons and work camps until 1956. His experiences there formed the basis for much of his writing.

The Olympic Boycott

The 1980 Summer Olympics were held in Moscow. These were the first Olympic Games in Eastern Europe. Instead of being a showcase for international sportsmanship and goodwill, the competition was marred by the politics of the Cold War. After the Soviet Union invaded Afghanistan in 1979, U.S. president Jimmy Carter warned that the United States would boycott the games if the USSR did not withdraw its troops. The Soviets ignored the warning, and the United States and other many nations, including Japan, China, Israel, Canada, and West Germany, refused to participate in the Olympics. Four years later, the Soviet Union boycotted the Summer Olympics in Los Angeles, California, claiming the United States was promoting anti-Soviet feelings around the world.

Sports

Sports have always played an important role in Russian life, especially after the 1917 revolution. The government poured millions of dollars into sports and physical training programs in an effort to create the world's best athletes. As a result, during the Soviet era, teams from the USSR won the most medals in fourteen of the eighteen Olympic Games in which they competed.

Gymnasts Svetlana Khorkina (1979–) and Olga Korbut (1955–) became international celebrities after achieving success at the Olympics. Khorkina participated in three Winter Olympics, winning seven medals. Korbut won six medals at

Olga Korbut was a top Soviet gymnast. She won three gold medals at the 1972 Olympics and one at the 1976 Olympics.

two Olympics. Strongman Vasily Alekseyev (1942–2011) was a world-class weight lifter, winning two gold medals in Olympic competition.

Ice hockey and tennis are also played widely in Russia. The Soviet ice hockey team has won seven gold medals in Olympic competition, and there are roughly thirty Russian-born players in the National Hockey League (NHL). In tennis, Russian superstars Maria Sharapova (1987–) and Dinara Safina (1986–) have each been ranked number one worldwide in women's professional tennis.

Alexander Ovechkin

Alexander Ovechkin is known as Ovi or "Alexander the Gr8" by his countless fans. He is one of the National Hockey League's (NHL) greatest stars. Born in Moscow into a family of athletes, he played four years (2001–2005) with the Dynamo Moscow team of the Russian Superleague. There, he led his team to a gold medal at the World Junior Championships. In 2005, Ovi joined the Washington Capitals of the NHL and made an immediate splash by winning the Calder Memorial Trophy for best rookie in the league. In 2008, he led the league in scoring with 112 points and became the first player in NHL history to win four major awards in one season: the Hart Memorial Trophy for most valuable player (MVP), the Lester B. Pearson Award (now named the Ted Lindsay Award) for MVP as voted by players, the Maurice Richard Trophy for most goals scored, and the Art Ross Trophy for most points scored. Ovi won the Hart Trophy again, in 2009, for scoring a league-leading 56 goals.

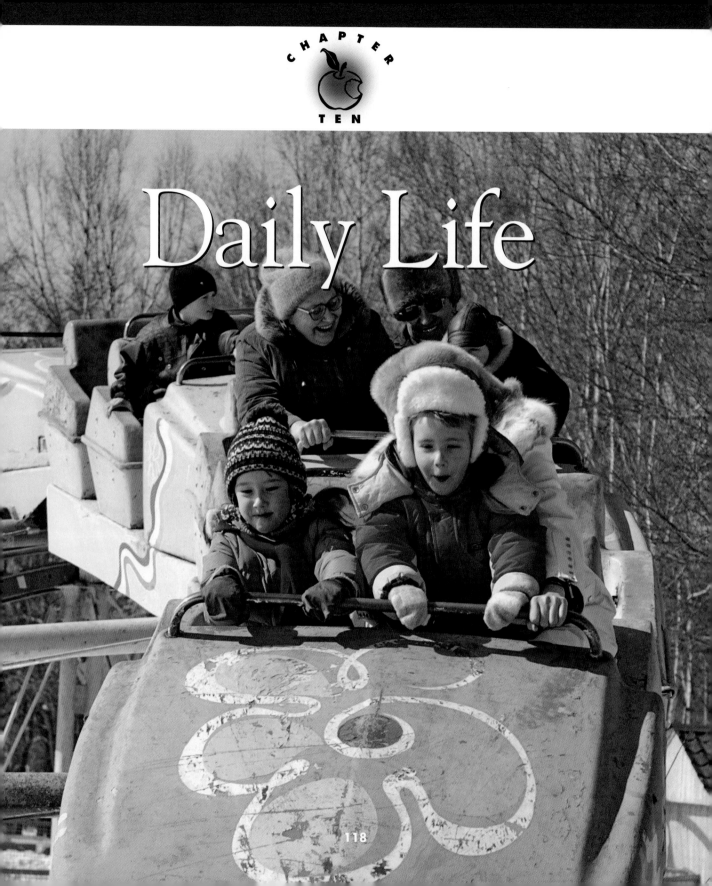

Daily Life

RUSSIA IS ONE OF THE MOST SPARSELY POPULATED nations in the world. It has an average population density of just 22 people per square mile (8.5 people per sq km). This is because few people live in large swaths of frozen Siberia. In 1950, 45 percent of Russia's population lived in urban areas. Today, roughly 75 percent lives in urban settings. During the 1950s and early 1960s, many Russians left the countryside to move to cities, where they hoped to earn a better living. The result was an urban housing shortage that exists to this day.

Opposite: Families enjoy a ride on an old roller coaster on the island of Sakhalin, off the eastern coast of Russia.

City Life

Most city residents live in small apartments in high-rise buildings. The living conditions are usually cramped, often with large families packed into small or medium-sized apartments. More than five million people live in communal apartments called *kommunalka*. This form of apartment living was started after the Bolshevik Revolution in 1917 to provide housing for the growing number of city dwellers. From two to seven families may share a kommunalka, with each family in one room.

About half of Russians living in large cities have a dacha, a modest second home located in the countryside. These homes were originally built by nobles, but were seized by the government after the Bolshevik Revolution. Some were made into vacation homes for workers, and many were given to high-ranking officials of the Communist Party. Today, wealthy Russians build multimillion-dollar dachas that have swimming pools, tennis courts, and even small forests and lakes on the property.

A dacha on Sakhalin Island

Speaking with Hands

Hand gestures and body language have different meanings in different parts of the world. Here are some common Russian hand gestures and their meanings:

Slapping your fingers on the center of your forehead	"That was dumb"
Making a cutting motion across your throat	"I've eaten enough"/"I'm full"
Pointing to the ceiling	"Someone could be listening"
Crossing your hands behind your back	Shows you are breaking a promise (similar to Americans crossing their fingers)
Thumbs up	Considered an insult

Country Life

During the Soviet era, the government owned most of the nation's land. Small farms were merged into large collectives. Farmworkers could not leave the land and were paid low wages.

After the fall of the USSR, the government offered to sell farmers the land they worked on. But few could afford to purchase it. Many people moved to cities. The lucky few who were able to buy the land amassed huge tracts. Many of them joined together to create successful corporations that manage the farms.

For those less fortunate, rural life in Russia is dying. Farmers who once worked on the government collectives have little or

Small farming villages are scattered across the steppe.

A Tasty Wedding Custom

Newlywed couples in Russia have an interesting way of determining who the head of the household will be. During the wedding or at the reception, the bride and groom are given *karavay*, a small round loaf of bread. With a third person holding the bread, the bride and groom each take a bite from the loaf without using their hands. Whoever takes the bigger bite is considered the head of the family. The bread also symbolizes health, wealth, and long life.

no land. Many have lost the free housing and free education the government once supplied. Older workers in many rural regions are in poor health. Young people are leaving behind the decaying farmland and crumbling houses for large cities.

Russian Cuisine

With more than a hundred different ethnic groups living in the Russian Federation, Russia offers one of the world's most diverse cuisines. A typical Russian meal might begin with appetizers that include breads, cold meat, smoked fish, and vegetables such as tomatoes and cucumbers. Russians also enjoy caviar—salted fish eggs taken from wild sturgeon living in the Black and Caspian Seas.

Following a course of soup, a hot main meal might consist of a fish or meat dish served with vegetables. *Kholodets* is a dish of boiled pieces of spiced pork or veal cooked in a gelatin. It is served cold and usually accompanied by horseradish or mustard.

Two of Russia's most beloved dishes are *kasha* and *blini*. Kasha is a thick dish made from ground or whole grains, such as buckwheat, barley, or oats. Peas may sometimes be substituted for the grains. It is often flavored with sugar, butter, or gravy. Blini are made with flour and milk or water, and look like soft, fluffy pancakes. They are often topped with sour cream, honey, caviar, or butter.

Meat and cabbage pies are also favorites at the Russian dinner table. *Pirozhki* are small buns stuffed with a variety of fillings and baked or deep-fried in oil. The fillings include rice and boiled eggs, chopped boiled meat with onions, sautéed cabbage, sautéed fish, or a variety of other tasty treats.

The meal may be topped off with a variety of sweet dessert treats. *Tvorog* is a cottage cheese that is often garnished with

Favorite Soups

Soups have always been an important part of the Russian diet, enjoyed either as a main meal or as a side dish. *Okroshka* is a cold soup made with kvass, a drink made from rye bread. Meat or fish is cooked with a mild vegetable such as potatoes, carrots, or cucumbers, and a spicier vegetable such as green onions or dill. *Botvinya* is another cold soup, made with the leafy tops of vegetables, mustard, garlic, and horseradish. Kvass is then poured over the vegetables.

Shchi, or cabbage soup, is a hot dish that has been enjoyed by Russians for over one thousand years. The soup is made with cabbage, carrots, spicy herbs, and a sour flavoring such as apples, sauerkraut, or *smetana*, a heavy sour cream. Rye bread is often eaten with shchi. *Lapsha* is a noodle soup made with a broth of chicken, mushroom, or milk combined with wheat flour or buckwheat noodles. Russians adopted lapsha from the Tatars and it became a staple of their diet.

honey or berries. *Sirok*, which is similar to cheesecake, is basically tvorog coated in chocolate. *Zefir* is a marshmallow treat that may be made with walnuts, berries, or bananas.

Festivals

During the Soviet era, the government put severe restrictions on religious practices and on the celebration of religious holidays. As religious freedom has been increasing in recent years, many religious holidays are now experiencing a rebirth.

The Soviets replaced the abandoned religious holidays with ones that celebrated Communist ideals. The most important was known as October Revolution Day, celebrated from 1917 to 2005 on November 7. In 2005, President Vladimir

Celebrations of religious holidays have grown in recent years. Here, people dressed in traditional costumes go caroling from house to house at Christmastime.

Russian Public Holidays

New Year's Day	January 1
Christmas Day	January 7
Defender of the Fatherland Day	February 23
International Women's Day	March 8
Spring and Labor Day	May 1
Victory Day	May 9
Russia Day	June 12
National Unity Day	November 4

Putin reinstituted National Unity Day to replace October Revolution Day. National Unity Day had been celebrated from 1649 to 1917. It commemorated the Russian uprising that forced Polish invaders out of Moscow in 1612.

People in Yekaterinburg take part in Spring and Labor Day festivities.

Soldiers march in a parade on Victory Day, which commemorates the end of World War II.

Spring and Labor Day, celebrated on May 1, was known as International Workers' Day in Soviet Russia. It was celebrated with workers' parades, pro-government demonstrations, and speeches given by officials of the Communist Party. Today, Russians use it primarily as a public holiday. Many people go to their dachas to do gardening or have family barbeques or picnics.

Victory Day, May 9, honors those who died in Russia's victory over Germany in World War II and pays tribute to survivors and veterans. It is one of Russia's most important national holidays. Local military parades and fireworks displays are held throughout the country. Crowds fill the streets, and Russian war veterans wear their uniforms and medals. The nation's largest celebration takes place at Moscow's Red Square. Schools often feature assemblies at which children sing wartime songs and tell stories about brave Russian soldiers.

Despite their uncertain future, Russians have shown themselves to be survivors. Throughout their turbulent history, they have overcome countless challenges and threats. As democracy continues to take root, Russians are hopeful that their nation will be transformed into a free and prosperous society for all who live there.

People enjoying a beautiful afternoon in St. Petersburg

Timeline

Russian History

Eastern Slavic tribes migrate into what is now Russia.	ca. 300 CE
Rurik becomes the leader of the Eastern Slavs, called the Rus.	862
The Rus capital moves to Kiev.	882
Vladimir I accepts Orthodox Christianity as the state religion.	988
Mongols begin their conquest of Kievan Rus.	1237
Mongols destroy Kiev and control Russia.	1240–1480
Ivan the Great unites the Russian principalities under his rule; he stops paying tribute to the Mongols.	ca. 1480
Ivan IV becomes First Czar of All the Russias.	1547
Czarist leaders become more oppressive during the Time of Troubles.	1598–1613
Michael Romanov becomes czar, beginning the Romanov dynasty.	1613
Peter the Great becomes czar and begins modernizing Russia.	1682
Catherine the Great is crowned empress and begins reform of Russia's law code.	1762

World History

ca. 2500 BCE	Egyptians build the pyramids and the Sphinx in Giza.
ca. 563 BCE	The Buddha is born in India.
313 CE	The Roman emperor Constantine legalizes Christianity.
610	The Prophet Muhammad begins preaching a new religion called Islam.
1054	The Eastern (Orthodox) and Western (Roman Catholic) Churches break apart.
1095	The Crusades begin.
1215	King John seals the Magna Carta.
1300s	The Renaissance begins in Italy.
1347	The plague sweeps through Europe.
1453	Ottoman Turks capture Constantinople, conquering the Byzantine Empire.
1492	Columbus arrives in North America.
1500s	Reformers break away from the Catholic Church, and Protestantism is born.

Russian History		World History
French emperor Napoléon Bonaparte invades Russia.	1812	
The Decembrists stage a failed revolt in St. Petersburg.	1825	
Alexander II frees the serfs, but little changes in the condition of Russian peasantry.	1861	1865 — The American Civil War ends.
		1879 — The first practical lightbulb is invented.
		1914 — World War I begins.
Peasants are massacred on Bloody Sunday.	1905	
Czar Nicholas II is overthrown; the Bolsheviks gain power.	1917	1917 — The Bolshevik Revolution brings communism to Russia.
The Union of Soviet Socialist Republics is formed.	1922	
The First Five-Year Plan calls for rapid industrialization and collectivization of all farms.	1929	1929 — A worldwide economic depression begins.
Millions of people are killed or exiled in massive purges.	1920s–1930s	
Germany attacks the USSR in World War II.	1941	1939 — World War II begins.
The Soviet army defeats the Germans at the Battle of Stalingrad.	1942–1943	1945 — World War II ends.
The USSR launches *Sputnik 1*, the world's first satellite, into orbit.	1957	1957 — The Vietnam War begins.
The Cuban missile crisis brings the USSR and the U.S. to the brink of nuclear war.	1962	1969 — Humans land on the Moon.
The USSR invades Afghanistan.	1979	1975 — The Vietnam War ends.
Soviet leader Mikhail Gorbachev announces the policies of *glasnost* and *perestroika*.	1985	1989 — The Berlin Wall is torn down as communism crumbles in Eastern Europe.
The USSR collapses.	1991	1991 — The Soviet Union breaks into separate states.
Russian military forces begin battling rebels in Chechnya.	1994	
Vladimir Putin is elected president.	2000	2001 — Terrorists attack the World Trade Center in New York City and the Pentagon near Washington, D.C.
		2004 — A tsunami in the Indian Ocean destroys coastlines in Africa, India, and Southeast Asia.
Dmitri Medvedev is elected president.	2008	2008 — The United States elects its first African American president.
Vladimir Putin is elected president.	2012	

Fast Facts

Official name: Russian Federation

Capital: Moscow

Official language: Russian

Moscow

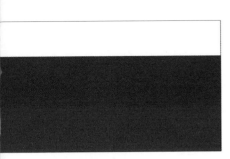

Russian flag

Volcanoes on Kamchatka Peninsula

Official religion:	None
Year of founding:	1991
National anthem:	"Gosudarstvenny Gimn Rossiyskoy Federatsii" ("National Anthem of the Russian Federation")
Type of government:	Federal republic
Chief of state:	President
Head of government:	Prime minister
Area of country:	6.6 million square miles (17 million sq km)
Latitude and longitude of geographic center:	Near Novosibirsk, 55°01' N and 82°56' E
Bordering countries:	Finland, Norway, Estonia, Latvia, Belarus, and Ukraine on the west; Georgia, Azerbaijan, Kazakhstan, China, Mongolia, and North Korea on the south; Kaliningrad bordered by Poland on the south and by Lithuania on the north and east
Highest elevation:	Mount Elbrus, 18,510 feet (5,642 m) above sea level
Lowest elevation:	Caspian Sea, 92 feet (28 m) below sea level
Average high temperature:	In St. Petersburg, 26°F (-3°C) in January, 73°F (23°C) in July
Average low temperature:	In St. Petersburg, 18°F (-8°C) in January, 59°F (15°C) in July
Average annual precipitation:	In the East European Plain, 24 to 28 inches (61 to 71 cm); in the western mountains, 79 inches (200 cm)

St. Basil's Cathedral

**National population
(2012 est.):** 143,056,383

**Population of major
cities (2010 est.):**

Moscow	11,514,330
St. Petersburg	4,848,700
Novosibirsk	1,473,737
Yekaterinburg	1,350,136
Nizhniy Novgorod	1,250,615

Landmarks:
- ▶ *Kremlin,* Moscow
- ▶ *St. Alexander Nevsky Cathedral,* Novosibirsk
- ▶ *St. Basil's Cathedral,* Moscow
- ▶ *State Hermitage Museum,* St. Petersburg
- ▶ *Winter Palace,* St. Petersburg

Economy: Russia has the seventh-largest economy in the world. Oil, natural gas, metals and minerals, and timber make up 80 percent of its exports. Machinery, aircraft, automobiles, iron and steel, and electronics are among its most important manufactured products. Russia is one of the world's largest producers of wheat.

Currency

Currency: The ruble. In 2011, 31 rubles equaled one U.S. dollar.

**System of weights
and measures:** Imperial system

Literacy rate (2006): 99.5%

Schoolchildren

Marc Chagall

Common Russian words and phrases:

zdravstvuite	hello
Kak dela?	How are you?
da	yes
nyet	no
spasibo	thank you
udachi	good luck
dasvidaniya	good-bye

Prominent Russians:

Mikhail Baryshnikov (1948–)
Ballet dancer

Catherine the Great (1729–1796)
Empress

Marc Chagall (1887–1985)
Painter

Vladimir Lenin (1870–1924)
Revolutionary, first Soviet head of state

Peter the Great (1672–1725)
Czar Peter I

Aleksandr Pushkin (1799-1837)
Poet

Leo Tolstoy (1828–1910)
Novelist, short story writer

To Find Out More

Books

▶ Davenport, John C. *The Bolshevik Revolution*. New York: Chelsea House, 2010.

▶ Price, Sean. *Ivan the Terrible: Tsar of Death*. New York: Franklin Watts, 2008.

▶ Sepetys, Ruta. *Between Shades of Gray*. New York: Philomel Books, 2011.

▶ Zu, Vincent. *Catherine the Great: Empress of Russia*. New York: Franklin Watts, 2009.

DVDs

▶ *Russian Revolution in Color*. Shanachie, 2007.

▶ *Russia's Last Tsar*. National Geographic, 2010.

▶ Visit this Scholastic Web site for more information on Russia:
www.factsfornow.scholastic.com
Enter the keyword **Russia**

Index

Page numbers in *italics*
indicate illustrations.

Meet the Author

NEL YOMTOV IS AN AWARD-WINNING AUTHOR and editor with a passion for writing nonfiction books for young people. Bitten by the reading bug at an early age, he learned how books could be the doorway to the wonders of our world and its people. Writing gives him the opportunity to investigate the subjects he loves and share his discoveries with young readers. In recent years, he has written books about history and geography as well as graphic-novel adaptations of classic mythology, military history, sports biographies, and science.

Yomtov was born in New York City. After graduating from college, he worked at Marvel Comics where he handled all phases of comic book production. By the time he left seven years later, he was supervisor of the product development division of Marvel's licensing program. Yomtov has also written, edited, and colored hundreds of Marvel comic books.

He has served as editorial director of a children's nonfiction book publisher and also as executive editor of the Hammond World Atlas book division. In between, he squeezed in a two-year stint as consultant to Major League Baseball, where he helped supervise an educational program for elementary and middle schools throughout the country.

Yomtov lives in the New York area with his wife, Nancy, a teacher and writer. His son, Jess, is a writer and radio broadcaster. Yomtov spends his leisure hours on the softball fields in New York City's Central Park and at neighborhood blues clubs playing harmonica with local bands.

Photo Credits